Feeding your Child with Autism

TOPICS IN AUTISM

Feeding your Child with Autism

A FAMILY-CENTERED GUIDE TO MEETING THE CHALLENGES

Mark J. Palmieri, Psy.D., BCBA-D & Kristen M. Powers, M.S., OTR/L

Sandra L. Harris, Ph.D., series editor

Woodbine House ◆ 2013

Published in the United States of America by Woodbine House,
Inc., 6510 Bells Mill Road, Bethesda, MD 20817. 800-843-7323.
www.woodbinehouse.com

Library of Congress Cataloging-in-Publication Data

Palmieri, Mark J.
  Feeding your child with autism : a family-centered guide to meeting the challenges
/ Mark J. Palmieri, Psy. D., BCBA & Kristen Powers, M.S., OTR/L. -- First edition.
     pages cm
  Includes bibliographical references and index.
  ISBN 978-1-60613-012-4
  1. Autism in children--Diet therapy. 2. Autistic children--Nutrition. 3. Parents of
autistic children. I. Powers, Kristen. II. Title.
  RJ506.A9P25 2013
  618.92'85882--dc23

                                                                              2013001157

Manufactured in the United States of America

10   9   8   7   6   5   4   3   2   1

To all the families whose endless effort and care have brought success to so many children

Table of Contents

Preface

Food is such an essential part of our lives, not only for the nutrition that sustains us, but also for the rituals that meals create. From birthday celebrations and holiday dinners to relaxing Sunday breakfasts, many of our favorite memories are shaped by the foods that are shared with family and friends. For many children with an autism spectrum disorder, however, meals are a source of challenge and conflict, and family members struggle to find ways to include adequate nutrition and to create an environment that is nurturing and supportive.

With the many advances in the treatment of autism spectrum disorders in the past forty years, we understand how to support children and to facilitate their participation and achievement in a variety of daily life skills. However, feeding continues to remain an area of critical importance and need for so many families. Families have expressed to us their concerns and fears, but also their hopes and their goals, even if only to take a family vacation together and have their son be able to eat in a different setting than he is used to. Through the years we have listened to many families share their stories and we have learned immensely from the parents, grandparents, nannies, and children who each have their own unique voice in their families, all of whom are reflected in this book.

As authors, we each provide a different perspective on treating individuals with autism spectrum disorders and feeding challenges. As a psychologist, understanding feeding difficulties requires behavioral assessment that determines the individual's needs and the functionality of the food refusal in order to establish an evidence-based treatment approach. As an occupational therapist, the emphasis is on the underlying physical and sensory-motor difficulties that interfere with eating, concentrating on oral-motor challenges, sensory sensitivities, and the postural stability and control required for effective and safe eating. Together, we present a comprehensive and evidence-based view of the child and family system in relation to eating.

The authors would like to thank the families that submitted pictures for the book, including the D'Eramo family, the Bordner family, the Burke family, the Azimova family, the Kelly family, and the Fleig family. We would like to extend our gratitude to our colleagues at The Center for Children with Special Needs. We would also like to thank the many parents and children who have taught us how to understand feeding challenges and how to treat them. We have worn many different flavors of yogurt over the years and have smiled through it all!

We would like to thank Nancy Gray Paul at Woodbine House for her support during the writing process, including answers to endless questions and clarifications on the smallest of details. Kristen would like to thank Michael and her stepsons, Seth and Evan, for their support, and Kaden, Tiernan, and Callen for the enthusiasm and joy that they bring to her life. Kristen would also like to thank her Haddam friends and her colleagues at RSD 17 for their never-failing ability to see the bright side while the book was being written. Mark would like to thank Sandra Harris and Michael Powers for their years of guidance, support, and mentorship. Together, we express special gratitude to our parents and friends for their support and encouragement during the writing—and rewriting—process.

1 | Beginning the Discussion: Feeding and Autism Spectrum Disorders

Introduction

The challenges faced by people with autism spectrum disorders (ASD) and their families are as diverse as the disorders themselves. Despite the hallmark delays in social interaction, language, and the specific interfering behaviors, the appropriate intervention services are highly individualized, ever-changing, and ongoing. When faced with the myriad of challenges, families often do not know where to begin. But if your child has feeding challenges in addition to autism, you're faced with frustration and anxiety at every mealtime and there's undoubtedly an urgency to your search for appropriate interventions and solutions.

Feeding difficulties cause extreme stress for children with ASD and create profound insecurities for the whole family unit. Understandably, parents fear the broad health implications of poor nutrition and struggle to cope with the dramatic interruptions feeding limitations place on the entire family. Many families worry that attempting to intervene with the feeding process will cause further—and more dangerous—eating restrictions. Many more feel that there is simply little that can be done to support change. In the face of serious social and communication delays, addressing such a core daily need as feeding can feel impossible and extremely nerve-racking, particularly for parents.

The goal of this book is to provide essential information for families to help them understand feeding disorders, consider the kinds of supports they can use at home, and the types of resources they should consider accessing in their communities. The model presented will emphasize a family-centered approach, including how such an approach can be integrated within community assessment and treatment. This book is also for you if you are someone who works with or supports people with ASD, including pediatricians, pediatric gastroenterologists, occupational therapists (OT), speech and language pathologists (SLP), board certified behavior analysts, feeding specialists, nutritionists, and dietitians.

Feeding disorders will be discussed with specific attention given to the many different factors often associated with them. Some of these will include meal-time rituals, food selectivity, oral-motor deficits, and aversions to particular food-related sensations such as mixed-texture aversions. When families report feeding difficulties, they are often referring to the challenging behaviors associated with food refusal, for example screaming, hitting others, and running from the table. These behaviors must be understood as only one part of the feeding challenge for any individual. Other difficulties commonly include feeding restrictions that follow from over-adherence to routines and highly rule-governed behavior. For example, a child who will eat particular foods only on certain days and in specific locations may demonstrate feeding rigidity. When these rules are violated, the child may experience significant behavioral dysregulation, resulting in any number of challenges.

Early indications of feeding challenges might include:

- Whimpering when new foods are presented
- Repeatedly requesting the same foods over and over
- Demanding that particular mealtime routines be followed over and over
- Pushing foods away
- Spitting out food
- Pursing the lips to refuse entrance of food
- Acting out physically at mealtimes, e.g., kicking, screaming, hitting
- Escaping from the table during mealtimes
- Gagging at the sight or smell of a particular food
- Vomiting with food presentation or ingestion
- Anger when other people eat different foods (than the child) at a meal
- Flopping out of the chair during mealtimes

- Pushing foods to different sides of the plate
- Separating foods when they are presented as a mixed group
  (e.g., peas and carrots)

There are many commonalities between the features of an autism spectrum disorder and typical characteristics of feeding restrictions. For example, individuals with ASD experience ritualized responding such as following very particular routines—placing materials (utensils, plates, or food) in specific ways or locations, and using items in a very prescribed fashion. For people with ASD and feeding restrictions, nonfunctional rituals are often associated with food or, more broadly, mealtimes. For ex-ample, some will drink from only one cup or eat certain foods in only one location. Individuals with ASD may also experience challenges with the sensory features of different environments (Keen, 2008). For example, a child may avoid entering rooms that are overly loud. With respect to feeding, these difficulties are generally associated with the food's smell, taste, texture, or temperature. Additionally, the general environment in which the food is served may be an issue. For example, a child may avoid eating in a school cafeteria because of the noise level or the smell of the many foods cooked there each day.

This book will discuss children with all types of behavioral challenges associated with nonorganic feeding disorders (without a biological cause) and will illustrate how to objectively observe these behaviors, how to understand them functionally, and to ultimately develop supportive interventions to address them. Regardless of the associated challenging behavior (e.g., spitting, crying, screaming), the goal will be to identify the underlying cause and develop a treatment to address the root of the challenge. For example, a child who screams when presented with new foods because of sensitivities to their appearance and smell will require interventions to help accommodate these sensory experiences and teach him to functionally communicate with others in these times of discomfort. Our emphasis here will be to provide information on common problems associated with the broad category of feeding disorders and then address a functional approach to developing person-centered interventions.

With respect to such interventions, this book will inform on the types of information caregivers should hope to gain from providers, the value of taking a functional perspective to assessment and treatment, and the various types of intervention commonly used, from home supports to more intensive and controlled treatment models. The information provided here will offer families a roadmap for beginning the process of understanding their children's needs with respect to feeding and for sifting through the various intervention strategies that may be helpful. In doing so, we hope to provide caregivers with the information necessary to understand the diversity of challenges associated with feeding limitations and the kind of help they should expect to gain from community-based treatments. These are treatments families access from local providers (without hospitalization) who offer expertise in feeding challenges and ASD. Typically, these services are provided in-home or in outpatient clinics by clinicians such as occupational therapists, behavior analysts, speech and language pathologists, or psychologists.

When discussing any intervention, we will strongly emphasize the importance of the family's role in supporting treatment. We'll include information on how families can participate in the assessment and treatment process and what indications they may look for to assess if meaningful and lasting change has been established.

Prevalence of Feeding Disorders

Feeding problems are not unique to children with autism spectrum disorders. They are reported to occur in approximately a quarter of the general population, with the vast majority of individuals ultimately outgrowing these challenges and eating a fairly typical diet. Among children with developmental disabilities, however, prevalence rates are much higher; reported as affecting from 60 to as much as 80 percent of the population (Burklow et al., 1998; Keen, 2008; Kerwin et al., 2005; Williams et al., 2000). Among those people with ASD and feeding difficulties, families report great diversity in the challenges experienced (Schreck et al., 2004). Some parents report food selectivity based on types of presentation including specific utensils, locations, and times of day. Others indicate that texture restrictions to pureed or smooth types of food are the most prominent concern. Preference restrictions with texture are often further complicated by sensitivities to food flavors or temperatures (Kuschner et al., 2005). Still others find that the narrow range of foods eaten, though they may be accepted in a variety of places and styles, makes feeding a major challenge.

What Kinds of Feeding Challenges Will This Book Address and Not Address?

The targeted feeding challenges addressed in this book relate to children with nonorganic feeding disorders commonly associated with autism spectrum disorders, such as rituals around feeding, oral-motor skill deficits, food selectivity, and learned maladaptive behaviors related to eating. (Nonorganic feeding disorders are best understood as those feeding issues that do not have a biological cause.) As such, this book will not describe interventions for those children with medically-based feeding challenges, including reflux, dysphagia, celiac disease, allergies, and food intolerance. Nor will it address the challenges faced by children with eating disorders such as anorexia or bulimia. However, individuals with these conditions may have co-occurring food selectivity, rigidities, or other limitations that may be helped by the information in this book. The interventions described in the book will not treat food allergies or swallowing difficulties; however, they may be relevant to address advancing a person's food repertoire.

Anorexia nervosa is a disorder wherein the affected individual is afraid of gaining weight and refuses to eat in order to avoid gaining weight (DSM-IV). Bulimia describes a disorder wherein the affected individual binge eats and uses methods of self-induced vomiting, diuretics, fasting, and extreme exercise to maintain his weight (DSM-IV). Both anorexia and bulimia involve misperception of body image and weight (DSM-IV) and, although nonorganic in origin, will not be discussed in this book.

Similarly, pica is a condition that will not be addressed in this book, despite the fact that it can be associated with pervasive developmental disorders (PDD) as well as intellectual disability (formerly mental retardation) (DSM-IV). Pica is described as persistently eating nonfood items for at least one month (DSM-IV). However, there are typically no food aversions that are associated with pica as would commonly be evident with a feeding disorder. For families of children with anorexia nervosa, bulimia, or pica, ongoing intervention should be led by their pediatrician and supported by a psychologist/psychiatrist as determined by their pediatrician.

Then there are those children who suffer from issues and conditions that affect eating that are organic in nature, i.e., having a biological cause. There are conditions that need to be ruled out before it can be determined that your child has a feeding problem that can be addressed by the advice in this book. These conditions include reflux, dysphagia, celiac disease, allergies, and food intolerance.

Reflux occurs when the contents from the stomach leak back into the esophagus after eating, causing discomfort, nausea, or even difficulty swallowing. Consequently, children with reflux often willfully avoid eating to prevent the subsequent discomfort experienced with eating. Children with a diagnosis of reflux would clearly benefit from medical intervention, first and foremost, to address the underlying medical condition.

Dysphagia is another medical condition that effects eating. Dysphagia is defined as difficulty swallowing and can be the result of medical conditions such as a brain injury or stroke. Dysphagia can be a condition itself and can impact nutrition and safe swallowing without choking. Families with children with dysphagia report a history of frequent upper respiratory infections, including pneumonia, coughing while eating, and even choking. However, some children do not present with obvious choking or signs of aspiration and thus dysphagia can be more difficult for families and service providers to detect.

Dysphagia is typically ruled out during a feeding evaluation and before intervention has been implemented. Sometimes, more extensive evaluation may be necessary to determine the presence of such swallowing deficits. A Modified Barium Swallow Study or a Videofluoroscopic Swallow Study may be recommended by the feeding team and pediatrician. These procedures are performed by a speech and language pathologist and a radiologist in a hospital setting. These studies will provide information on the consistency of the food that is safe for the child, such as pureed or ground consistency, and any postural modifications, such as head positioning while eating to promote a safe swallow, including a chin tuck with a swallow. Once the most effective plan for safe and effective swallowing has been determined, feeding intervention can begin. Without full diagnostic evaluation, however, a feeding team cannot begin intervention if there is a concern regarding swallowing.

Some children with feeding difficulties present with physical discomfort following eating. These children may need to be evaluated by their pediatrician for the presence of any potential medical condition, including food allergies. As noted with reflux, some children may restrict their eating if they associate eating with subsequent physical discomfort. Food allergies are described as an immune system response as the body reacts to the food as a harmful trigger and tries to fight the food itself. Food allergies can range from benign responses, such as itching and hives, to severe reactions, such as swelling in the mouth and throat that can lead to difficulty breathing or anaphylaxis. Children with especially severe allergies need to understand their food limitations and should carry an EpiPen® in case they unknowingly eat a trigger food. Allergies are diagnosed by an allergist and a specific treatment plan is designed to accommodate these challenges.

Celiac disease is another medical condition that should be ruled out before launching into a feeding treatment program. Celiac disease is an autoimmune disorder in which the lining of the small intestine is damaged and prevents it from absorbing nutrients from food. The damage is caused by gluten in the diet, which is found in wheat, barley, and rye. Symptoms include but are not limited to weight loss, failure to thrive in children, diarrhea, constipation, abdominal bloating, and fatigue. The only treatment is the elimination of gluten from the individual's diet.

Max's mother is frustrated. She sees that five-year-old Max becomes cranky after meals and often has a distended stomach. He has frequent diarrhea and constantly complains of stomachaches. While he was recently diagnosed with an autism spectrum disorder, she feels that some of his behavioral difficulties must be related to his stomach problems. She has complained repeatedly to the pediatrician, who did have him tested for celiac disease, though the test came back negative. Max was also evaluated by an allergist who told Max's mom that Max does not have an identifiable allergy to any food. She has recently begun to keep a food diary of all of the foods that Max eats and the resulting stomach symptoms that he presents with to see if there is any relationship between the foods that Max eats and his symptoms.

Food intolerance has received much attention lately as more and more people are describing an increase in digestive problems, including abdominal cramps, diarrhea, and bloating. Food intolerance is different from allergies in that there is often no easy way or medical test to identify these intolerances. Parents are often required to keep a food log to identify any correlation between their child's symptoms and the consumption of a particular food. A food intolerance is often identified when a particular food is excluded from the diet (for a sufficient amount of time) and the result is a reduction or elimination of symptoms.

Since many children with autism spectrum disorders lack the ability to articulate their discomfort, a food intolerance can be challenging for caregivers to easily identify. Lactose and, more recently, gluten are two of the more common intolerances typically reported by parents and caregivers. It is important for any food intolerances to be identified before the feeding team begins intervention since the child may limit his intake of any foods in the presence of underlying stomach discomfort. The feeding team will need to incorporate any dietary modifications (including eliminating any potential trigger foods) into their intervention plan at the onset of therapy to promote integration of these foods into the repertoire that the child will eat.

A controversial approach to the management of ASD has been the elimination of casein and gluten from the child's diet. Gluten, as noted, is found in wheat and other grains, including rye and barley. Casein is a protein found in milk and foods containing milk, such as yogurt, cheese, and butter. While not widely supported by the medical and behavioral community, advocates of a gluten and casein free (GF/CF) diet claim that some people with autism cannot digest gluten and casein, ultimately contributing to behavioral problems and exacerbating speech difficulties. There is little evidence-based support for this type of approach to addressing ASD unless there is a true allergy or intolerance to these types of foods. Additionally, for children with food selectivity issues, removing more foods from their diets without a medical need may further restrict their overall food repertoire, affecting adequate nutritional intake. To ensure adequate nutritional intake, it is important for families concerned about casein and gluten in their child's diet to discuss their concerns with their pediatrician and a dietician before removing these foods.

Health Concerns

Given the pressures on the family, the complexity of developmental disabilities, and the nutritional and social impact of feeding deficits, there is a critical need in the community for comprehensive, evidence-based, treatment approaches that support lifelong improvements. Without such intervention, a person with a feeding disorder is likely to experience longstanding limitations that encompass both nutrition and other feeding-related factors.

With respect to nutrition, children with food selectivity limit their overall repertoire of food choices. This can mean restrictions in necessary food groups such as fruits, vegetables, and proteins—all essential for growth and development. Families report many concerns about their children's nutrition and the impact of deficits on daily functioning. Importantly, these include difficulties participating in activities of daily living, education, and community life. Perhaps most prominent among these is family and school concerns regarding attention and focus. Children with feeding restrictions are often described as "unavailable for learning." In many cases, teams report that these children struggle to follow directions and sustain participation in activities for an appropriate amount of time. Also, teams report that children exhibit visible signs of fatigue such as slouching in their chairs, falling asleep, putting their heads down on their desks, and limited participation in physical activities.

Difficulties participating in activities of daily living, education, and community life are typical concerns about children with autism spectrum disorders; however, they are markedly more profound when a feeding disorder co-occurs. At home, parents describe that their children are more likely to select sedentary activities such as watching

TV or playing on the computer after going to school for the day. They report that it is difficult to engage their children in activities for periods of more than a few minutes. Their concerns also include worries that energy seems to come in short bursts. For example, after having a snack consisting of sugars or other carbohydrates, such as a slice of cake, their children may head outside for a short period but soon return to graze on more snacks.

In addition to concerns about energy and attention, parents worry about the risk of increased illness when their child doesn't eat a healthy diet. While they may not have "buy-in" from their pediatrician about a direct relationship between dietary concerns and illness, they do find that, experientially, their children with food restrictions are more prone to illness. Additionally, it is very common for a family to find that immediately after recovering from a cold or stomach illness, their child has dropped certain foods from his already limited diet. This may be related to the interruption in diet due to cold symptoms such as a stuffy nose or upset stomach or due to the pairing of painful symptoms with eating certain foods. For example, if a chicken nugget was the last thing a child ate before vomiting, this could influence his choice to avoid it in the future. These and other feeding-related issues will be discussed further in later chapters.

An Argument for Early Intervention with Feeding

Feeding restrictions have a significant impact on all levels of development. Importantly, children with feeding restrictions who do not undergo treatment are more likely to suffer from medical issues that result from poor nutrition (Clark et al., 1993). So often, families find that this does not become a major priority for the child until he reaches adolescence, by which time rigidity around food has become quite ingrained. Additionally, the accommodations necessary to address nutritional deficits (e.g., taking vitamins, drinking supplements) become extremely cumbersome by this stage. Waiting until this age to address nutritional concerns might also be due to the fact that many other priorities for intervention (e.g., speech) overshadow feeding when a child is young. However, the impact of leaving feeding deficits untreated is profound and typically more difficult to address as the child ages. For example, adolescents are generally expected to develop independence with feeding and self-management. Those who have highly restricted feeding repertoires face many challenges in this regard.

Treatment Options

The impact of feeding issues on individuals with developmental disabilities and their families is profound, though few treatment options are available to address these difficulties. Occupational therapists and speech and language pathologists might work with your child to address the underlying oral-motor skill deficits or sensory challenges that may be associated with his feeding challenges. Additionally, behavioral treatments conducted at inpatient facilities, schools, or community outpatient treatment centers offer help and support for struggling families.

Occupational therapists and speech and language pathologists employ techniques to improve lip mobility, chewing abilities, and tongue control to more effectively manage food and liquids once they are in the child's mouth. These types of interventions may incorporate some principles of behavior modification into their therapies, but often these interventions are not data-driven. Successful treatment of feeding disorders is improved with the use of an integrated treatment approach that incorporates evidence-based decision making. For example, a comprehensive treatment team may include both an occupational therapist and a board certified behavior analyst.

Additionally, many occupational therapists use sensory-based interventions, including playing with food, and oral-motor stimulation to address sensory issues but often they do not introduce food in a systematic presentation or even introduce it at all. Although these techniques may be enjoyable and even motivating to the child, they may not ultimately advance food acceptance. These sensory-based interventions lack empirical support and the child is not typically guided through the use of clearly defined treatment plans. Nor is individualized data collection used to evaluate gains to define treatment parameters. For these reasons, we advocate strongly for interventions that are grounded in data that demonstrate their effectiveness, and use a multi-disciplinary approach incorporating strategies to treat behavioral challenges and oral-motor limitations as appropriate.

Inpatient treatment centers for behavioral restructuring often involve having the child and caregiver move to the hospital or other treatment center for a period of time while therapy is completed multiple times daily. Such treatment may involve behavior analysts and medical staff to supervise the interventions and offer information to the family. After a period of weeks, the child is generally discharged and the family endeavors to take what has been learned in the center and apply it to life at home.

School and community programs for feeding disorders take place on an outpatient basis, with patients being seen regularly (i.e., weekly) in a therapeutic setting. Behavioral approaches typically emphasize treatment of rigid food refusals, aversion to certain features of food, and skills that the child lacks (e.g., communicating preferences). Often these interventions are limited with respect to oral-motor concerns. Community interventions may include periodic direct treatment with the child and some education for family members and other caregivers on how to support skill practice. The duration and intensity of these treatments varies greatly. More about these treatment options will be discussed in Chapters 6 and 7.

The Family-Centered Team Approach

Feeding difficulties present complex treatment challenges for parents. When feeding challenges first present, parents will often attempt to remedy the issue at home before turning to community supports, such as outpatient therapists. When this is unsuccessful they may look to individuals already working with their child on other issues such as a Board Certified Behavior Analyst (BCBA) or their child's special educator. Parents often find it challenging to identify the appropriate clinicians to work with their child and, when they do find one that can help, successfully transferring treatment methods to multiple environments is usually difficult. Family members report great concerns with the development of treatment procedures because they often find that while some gains have been made, the improvements made outside of the therapeutic setting do not transfer to other settings, or the gains are lost in a short period following the end of treatment.

School teams, community therapists, private treatment centers, and home-based treatment providers often attempt to offer support as part of academic, speech and language, occupational, or behavioral therapy. Each practitioner may offer a different perspective to the family about the key elements contributing to the feeding difficulty (e.g., motor control, sensory aversions, behavioral rigidities). What may be lacking is an integrated approach that offers the necessary expertise and resources (e.g., treatment time, training time with caregivers) to address the specific challenges of feeding.

When developing therapeutic treatments for food restrictions we must address the person's needs as a whole. This means considering not only expanding the feeding repertoire but also the social interaction, communication, and behavioral flexibility skills necessary for feeding. This requires an approach that prioritizes comprehensive assessment and intervention planning in a way that follows gains through all parts of their generalization. In this book, we advocate for an evidence-based assessment and treatment approach that offers a model for studying the feeding disorder, defining its parameters, and moving forward with treatment in a way that is defined, evaluable, and transferable (able to be generalized to many environments). Again, an integrated treatment approach that relies upon the expertise of multiple disciplines and data-based decision making is necessary. We advocate for community-based interventions that utilize the principles of applied behavior analysis (ABA) to understand the function of food restrictions for the individual and address the underlying oral-motor foundation for overall food acceptance.

An evidence-based approach to treating feeding disorders will require the feeding treatment team to be prepared to communicate with family members, the school team, and other community practitioners to help coordinate treatment. This feature of feeding interventions is often omitted from treatment models; however, without it, the risk for limited gains is quite high. For example:

> *A mother reports that her nine-year-old child has had problems with feeding since he was two years old. When he was seven, a behavior analyst started working with his school team and together they agreed to help treat the feeding challenges at school. Her son participated in a fading procedure where new foods were slowly introduced and he was given rewards for complying with directions. Also, his feeding-related challenging behaviors (hitting, screaming,*

and flopping to the floor) were redirected with a prompt back to his seat and representation of the demand. He made some gains and even began to eat ten new foods at school. The team described the procedures being used to the mother and provided her with videos of their work. As she attempted to present the foods at home, she saw some success. For example, her son would allow her to ask him to smell various foods. The gains at home, however, were slow and when the school year ended, the summer brought a complete loss to the gains. By the time the next school year started, the mother was hopeful that her son could improve his feeding abilities at school, but not optimistic that these gains would ever have lifelong impact.

The challenges faced by this mother help to illustrate how important it is for feeding interventions to address the immediate concerns with accepting new foods but also the lifelong concerns of stable and well generalized gains. Interventions must plan for sustainable, lasting change that is consistent across many settings.

Throughout this book, we will discuss the features of feeding disorders common to individuals with autism spectrum disorders, strategies families may use to help children struggling with feeding restrictions, as well as a model for community-based treatment that addresses behavioral and oral-motor limitations using sound, evidence-based practices. Our goal is for this book to help families and practitioners better conceptualize the feeding challenges experienced by people with autism spectrum disorders. In doing so, we aim to enable the reader to consider helpful strategies that may reduce these challenges and evaluate those treatment procedures being considered for use with any child.

Language to Know

Feeding disorders are often made more complex by the many clinical terms applied by different practitioners when assessing and treating them. The table below outlines specific terminology that will be used throughout the book and will be helpful to understanding how we describe feeding challenges and typical treatment procedures. Also, please note that we have alternated gender pronouns by chapter for ease's sake.

Common Terms Associated with Feeding Disorders and Treatments

Casein	A protein found in milk and milk products.	Griffin has a casein intolerance and is unable to eat any products containing milk, cheese, or cream.
Celiac disease	An autoimmune disorder that affects the lining of the small intestine in response to ingestion of gluten.	After a year of continual stomach complaints, Nathan was diagnosed with *celiac disease* and is unable to eat foods that contain gluten.
Data	This is any piece of specific information that is collected in order to help us better understand a situation or behavior. Data come in many forms but, importantly, all data should be clearly defined and collected reliably.	Rachel and her family are going to a weekly feeding clinic. At home she is working with her family on tasting three new foods. Her parents are collecting *data* each day on the time spent tasting, the number of bites she took, and if she picked up the food on her own.
Desensitization	This is a process by which a person becomes increasingly comfortable with something new. Typically, new experiences can be introduced slowly so that the person becomes progressively more comfortable with them. Over time, expectations are increased until the person achieves a typical and independent level of functioning.	Gloria has trouble with the smell of sautéed vegetables at home. She is first asked to smell them in a room near the kitchen while staying calm. Over time she is brought closer to the kitchen and then eventually tasked with staying in the kitchen for short periods. In time, the smell is no longer bothersome to her and she can stay in or pass through the kitchen with no difficulty.

(continued on next page)

Differential reinforcement	This is a process for using reinforcement to target a very specific behavior. Here one behavior may be selected to be rewarded while another similar behavior is not. This process is used often when trying to shape behavior.	Tyler has three ways of refusing food: throwing it, screaming, and saying, "No thank you." When he says, "No thank you," his father says, "Okay," and moves the food. When he screams or throws his food, his father does not say, "Okay," and the food is kept on the table. Here, "No thank you" is being *differentially reinforced.*
Gag reflex	A protective oral-motor reflex that can be persistent and exaggerated in the presence of underlying oral-motor deficits.	Tiernan exhibits a *gag reflex* when presented with foods that have a mixed consistency.
Generalization	The ability to transfer a skill learned in one environment to new environments. The goal is to help someone behave a certain way in all situations such as with different people, in different places, and with different materials.	Jeremy is able to eat a snack at school when sitting at his table, but will not eat a snack anywhere else. He is being taught to *generalize* this skill to eat a snack at tables in other classrooms.
Gluten	A protein composite found in foods that are processed from wheat and other similar grains, such as rye and barley.	Eli has very poor communication skills and has an intolerance to *gluten.* When he eats gluten he experiences pain. His feeding intervention team needs to teach him safe and unsafe foods for his diet.
Lip closure	The ability of the lips to work through the appropriate range of motion to help achieve a full closure of the lips while feeding, talking, or at rest.	Kaden is unable to achieve full *lip closure* around a spoon to adequately remove yogurt from the bowl of the spoon.

Motivation	This is a requirement for any of us to do anything. Motivation makes us want to do something. Sometimes motivators are introduced into an environment, for example, a prize for trying, and sometimes motivators occur naturally, for example, being sleepy or hungry makes us want to lie down or eat.	Zach's family has decided to work with him on feeding while at home. They have a special prize that Zach loves that is **only** available when they work on feeding. They make a point of practicing feeding when Zach is very likely to be hungry.
Muscle tone	The degree of tension within the muscle, which allows the muscle to react or respond to stretch. Abnormal muscle tone can be characterized as low muscle tone (hypotonia) or high muscle tone (hypertonia).	Evan demonstrates generalized low *muscle tone* as evidenced by a rounding in his shoulders, a dropped head, and a mildly protruding abdomen while standing.
Nuk™ brush	One of the oral-motor tools commonly used by occupational and speech therapists to address oral-motor skill development and tactile stimulation. The head of this tool is a rubber nub with flexible ridges that provides tactile input when applied to the oral structures. The tool is also used by parents with their infant child to get them used to tooth brushing.	The occupational therapist uses a *Nuk brush* to provide tactile stimulation to Colton's tongue prior to introducing food.

(continued on next page)

Term	Definition	Example
Postural stability	The ability of the trunk, head, and upper body to maintain a stable base of control for functional motor performance. It is dependent on efficient muscle tone, balance, strength, and awareness of the body in space for effective processing.	Andrew demonstrates decreased *postural stability* during feeding, which results in his resting his head on his hand and sliding forward in his chair while seated at the table.
Prompt	This is anything that is done to help someone complete a behavior. Prompts should be designed to decrease over time until a person is independent.	Cody is able to touch a fork that has food on it but can't yet move it all the way to his mouth. His parents give him a *prompt* by helping shape his hand around the fork and support his hand all the way to his mouth.
Proprioception	The sensory system that provides us with 'body in space' awareness. It receives information from the sensory receptors in our muscles and joints and is processed by the central nervous system.	Callen exhibits decreased *proprioceptive* awareness and tends to overstuff his mouth with food while eating to compensate.
Punishment	When you think of punishment, think the opposite to reinforcement. Punishment, simply, is anything done after a behavior that makes the behavior much less likely to happen again. Punishment is understood by its effect on someone, **not** primarily by our intention.	Natalia walked over to the table, picked up a piece of blue cheese, and smelled it. She did not enjoy this smell so in the future she was more resistant to going near any food on the table. Here the smell *punished* Natalia's exploration.
Reinforcement	Anything you do that makes some specific behavior more likely to occur again in the future. One of the most important things to remember	When presented with food Jimmy said, "Not now, maybe later." His father said, "Okay, bud, no problem," and removed the food. The next

	is that reinforcement is determined by how it affects someone, **not** by what our intention is. Giving something or taking something away can both be ways to reinforce something.	day Jimmy did the same thing so we know that his father *reinforced* him by taking away the food and praising his language.
Shaping	This is a process to slowly change a behavior into something much more sophisticated and functional. Step-by-step we help move a person's behavior closer and closer to what will be most helpful for him.	Maria would only come into the kitchen when her mother called her in for dinner. She was praised when she would walk in, but over time she was required to take one more step toward the table before she was praised. Eventually she had to sit in her seat before she was praised. In this manner, her behavior was *shaped*.
Stereotypic	This term is associated with any behavior that follows a very specific pattern. Such behaviors are often highly repetitive and follow a very predictable sequence. This term can describe behavior of any type such as vocalizations or other motor movements.	Carter will tap his chest rapidly and repeatedly with his spoon each time that he is told to eat. This is a *stereotypic* behavior in that it is highly predictable and looks extremely consistent over time.
Tactile	The sensory system of touch by which input is detected by receptors in the skin and processed by the central nervous system.	Nolan demonstrates an exaggerated response to unexpected *tactile* occurrences. For example, when a metal spoon touches his lips, he screams.

(continued on next page)

Texture	Refers to the consistency of presented foods, as well as the way the food items feel in the mouth.	Cal refuses to eat foods that have a lumpy texture, though he eats foods that have a smooth texture.
Texture fading	This is a common process in feeding treatments where a food is prepared to have a very particular, and consistent, texture and then is slowly adjusted until the texture is normal.	Margaret is working on eating peas. Initially, these were given to her fully mashed and now she is eating them chopped into very small pieces.
Tongue lateralization	The ability of the tongue to move from side to side in the mouth to bring foods from one side of the mouth to the other while eating.	During the occupational therapy evaluation, Julian did not demonstrate adequate tongue lateralization to move the bite of cracker from one side of his mouth to the other.
Toothette	A mouth swab that can be used in oral-motor and feeding programs.	Jonah likes to have the toothette swiped over his lips and cheeks.

2 The Impact of Feeding Problems on Everyday Life: Family, School & Community

While staring endlessly at the rows of chicken nuggets in the grocery store freezer, Luigi's mother wondered how it was possible that there were no more of the dino-shaped nuggets. In a world where one could find ten types of chicken nuggets in a single store, it seemed

impossible to her that each of the three grocery stores in her town were out of these particular nuggets. With a quick glance back to Luigi, she quickly abandoned the idea that he would somehow tolerate the standard rectangle-shaped nuggets and she mentally prepared for their trip to the stores in the next town over.

Luigi is a seven-year-old boy with a very complex history. He was diagnosed with autistic disorder at age two by a team of psychologists. His language was slow to develop but by now he is able to use basic phrases. He lives at home with his mother, father, nine-year-old brother, Mateo, and four-year-old sister, Pia. Luigi has been receiving intervention services since he was three years old. These include behavioral supports, occupational therapy, speech therapy, and physical therapy. His family is very pleased with Luigi's progress; however, his food restrictions continue to be extremely complicated. Even with all these interventions, Luigi has never made more than minimal gains in the area of eating. A few of his therapists have tried to support Luigi and his family with suggestions, but these rarely have had lasting impact.

Luigi's food restrictions started early on. He began to refuse to eat new foods at about three years of age. At that time, his mother and father noticed that there was a staple set of foods he enjoyed and that most other types were refused. Initially, while he would refuse new types of food, he would eat a number of different types of foods in certain categories. For example, he had no problem eating many different flavors of yogurt. Given Luigi's many issues at the time, his family did little to address these budding food restrictions. With all that Luigi struggled with (speech, playing, walking, fine motor skills) accommodating some picky eating seemed the least of their worries.

As the years pressed on and Luigi saw gains in many areas, his food restrictions became more and more prominent. What was once understood as "being a picky eater just like his father," became a highly scripted eating routine. He came to prefer certain brands (and balked if the packaging had changed) and refused similar foods of all other brands. Luigi also refused foods that had an unusual texture including those foods that were mixed or combined in texture.

While Luigi's parents didn't recognize the gentle trend evolve over time, by Luigi's seventh birthday it was evident that the problem had come to dominate much of their daily life. His parents felt as though one day they woke up to a life fraught with routine, completely centered around Luigi's eating behaviors.

At present, Luigi eats or drinks eleven foods regularly. These include Doritos®, dino-nuggets, French fries (from his favorite fast food chain), a particular brand of vanilla yogurt, plain bagels, Cheerios®, plain hamburger meat cooked in a skillet, milk, grape juice, watermelon, and apple sauce (store brand).

Like many families that have children with feeding issues, Luigi's parents have adjusted to accommodate Luigi's feeding needs in order to ensure that he is safe and healthy, and to avoid the challenges that inevitably result from pushing him. When Luigi's parents try to make Luigi eat something new, he refuses by flopping to the floor, screaming, spitting out food, gagging, and crying. Worse than that, they've found that any foods associated with such a tantrum (even ones that were previously tolerated) are often refused in the future. In order to ensure he will eat a consistent lunch at school (applesauce or yogurt, grape juice, and Doritos) and to increase stability at home, Luigi's parents have simply stopped pressing him.

Luigi's parents have friends and family who have learned what foods to have available and this has helped when attending birthday parties and other family events. However, even these are becoming more difficult as Luigi's other rituals associated with eating are becoming more and more prominent. For example, Luigi has developed a preference for a certain plate and spoon to use for eating, and will refuse to eat with any other plate or spoon.

In order to allow his brother and sister to spend time with friends and family, Luigi's mother and father have started to drive separate cars to family and community events. This allows one of them to leave on time to bring Luigi home for his meal (always allowing enough time for mealtime routines). They have even come to rely on the "two car strategy" when at close friends' homes in case the friends inadvertently purchased the wrong brand of tolerated food. It seems only fair to them that Luigi's brother and sister get to stay and that Luigi go home to eat. But even this solution is beginning to wear thin—Luigi's siblings have started to protest that one parent needs to leave in order to bring Luigi home.

At home, the challenges are growing beyond navigating Luigi's food-specific needs. His sister has taken to also requesting very specific foods (especially favorite snacks) instead of eating what has been cooked for the rest of the family. Seeing her brother's success getting what he wants, she acts in kind. The parents are modestly successful at redirecting her but not without anxiety and frustration.

As Luigi's mother turned to leave the store that didn't have the right type of dino-shaped nuggets in stock, she remembered that she hadn't yet heard back from the yogurt company. She had emailed them the week before because they had stopped making Luigi's favorite type of vanilla yogurt in the "correct" container. Her contingency plan to reuse the old container daily was fading with the ink on the side of the plastic container. She remembered that tonight was baseball practice for Mateo and that her husband would be taking him so that she could handle Luigi's dinner.

As she approached the car, she had a difficult time managing the anger she felt, including mounting anger toward the store and the food companies for not keeping their selections consistent. Given all the accommodations she has to make to keep Luigi's meals consistent, it seemed the least they could do.

We understand that feeding problems have a deep and broad impact on the family system. There are few aspects of daily life that are not affected by feeding issues. Whether it is the difficulty of planning meals or arranging for overnight stays, the necessity for a healthy and well generalized feeding routine is clear. As we consider the individual children who experience feeding disorders, we must remain aware of the underlying foundation that surrounds these children—their families—and begin our assessment and treatment planning process from this point.

Parents are often referred for feeding treatments following a conversation with their child's pediatrician where concerns are raised. These often include worries about weight, growth, and their child's overall nutritional profile. Concerns about weight might center around trying to help the child gain weight as well as being overweight. For those unfamiliar with feeding disorders, especially in people with autism, it is common to assume that being underweight is the main challenge; however, being overweight is quite typical. Many children with food restrictions eat diets that are heavy with sugars and other carbohydrates as well as high in fat. These high calorie foods (e.g., potato chips, chicken nuggets, French fries, bagels) are often noted as prominent contributory factors to weight issues. In addition, potential vitamin and mineral deficiencies may occur due to the over-selection of these restricted food choices. Taken together with the difficulties in attention and energy levels, a child with a feeding disorder can suffer from being overweight.

For others, their food restrictions mean that they take in an insufficient number of calories and so struggle to gain or maintain weight. Given these concerns, families often turn to nutritional supplements such as vitamins and pediatric enriched supplements like PediaSure© or Boost Kid©. Conversely, pediatricians, who are often unfamiliar with the complex behavioral profiles of children with autism, may fail to recognize the impact of food selectivity as a concern because the weight of the child may be within the normal range. However, this can cause long-term health complications if left untreated over time.

In addition to nutritional concerns, food selectivity and other food restrictions can be associated with health concerns such as poor dentition (teeth and gums). Often, compromised nutrition can be identified by health care providers other than your pediatrician, including dentists and school nurses, as they evaluate broader measures of health. Children with feeding limitations often experience significant difficulty acquiring dental hygiene skills due to tactile sensitivity both inside and outside of their mouths as well as other associated behavioral rigidities. For example, a child who struggles to tolerate the feeling of a toothbrush on her teeth and gums may develop a complicated set of refusal behaviors in order to ensure that this is avoided each morning and night. Furthermore, since kids with ASD often develop complex rituals that broadly impact their daily functioning, we must consider that feeding and oral hygiene routines are no less likely to be affected. Early on, these children may be highly resistant to the placement of a toothbrush, toothpaste, or even rinses into the mouth. This can result in a future of refusal to engage in personal dental hygiene and, over time, significantly affect personal health.

How do Feeding Challenges Affect Family Life?

Commonly, parents will note that they hadn't appreciated how challenging eating could be until their own child struggled. When one member of the family struggles to eat or to engage in any of the dozens of behaviors associated with sharing a meal, the entire family is affected and must adjust. For many families this means adopting many, often extremely complex, rituals that enable the member with feeding difficulties to eat something and still allows the family's day to move forward. All too often it is only after years of frustration, adjustments, and increasingly dangerous symptoms that families access support services.

Developing accommodating strategies is often the first step that families take to cope with feeding challenges. In all cases, these accommodations develop out of a need—whether it is to maintain basic nutrition, avoid destabilizing the family, devote resources to the countless other intervention priorities, or any of the other factors that play into supporting the child with autism and the entire family. (Although impossible to capture the full scope of these accommodations here, some of the most common are described below.) Just to get some food into their child, parents very often submit to cooking only particular types of foods, at certain times, and serving them in a very specific fashion. For example, a mother may learn through trial and error that a certain number of premade fish sticks, if heated appropriately so as to avoid any overly mush or crispy parts, could be successfully served to her daughter.

Families struggle extensively with feeding challenges, and regardless of the particular form of the challenges, we find that many families share similar stories about the impact of the feeding disorder on the family system. These concerns can, at times, be as detrimental to the social and emotional health of the child and the family as the physical and nutritional impact. In order to appropriately guide the assessment of needs and the development of treatment plans, the feeding team must take into consideration the impact of feeding issues on the family as a whole.

Below are some examples of experiences shared by families after they have adapted to the long-term impact of feeding limitations:

- **Restaurant limits**—Families report that there are only a few restaurants where they can successfully "enjoy" a meal. When there, they have to sit at the same table each time and follow several other rituals once they enter. For example, they must review the location of each bathroom before sitting down. Any deviation from expectations on the part of the child with autism results in yelling and refusing to sit, a complete refusal to eat, and eventually a tantrum. Assuming that all goes well and the family can sit to eat, they then must hope that there have been no changes in the way the favorite meal is prepared. The family waits with great anticipation for the hamburger (no bun, no vegetables, no cheese), for example, to arrive with the French fries. The plan is for the mother to intercept the plate, offer it a quick inspection, and move those French fries completely away from the hamburger before her son sees it. If this process goes well and no one orders a dish that is overly smelly or visually offensive, there is a good chance that the rest of the meal will proceed smoothly. The general mealtime anxiety experienced by all members of the family is not insignificant and results in ongoing stress and ultimately has a deep impact on the family's ability to positively spend time together.

- **Family celebration limits**—Holidays and other family celebrations become events of greater stress than would be expected due to feeding issues. Very often families cannot attend a full celebration because their child will not eat in new locations or will not tolerate others eating unfamiliar foods around her. Families report that while they have tried countless strategies to eat away from home, they have had no lasting success. Even bringing the food, plates, utensils, and a chair from home doesn't result in meaningful progress. Eventually the family adjusts, often by attending events either before or after meals, or by sending one adult home with the child with feeding issues while the rest of the family stays to eat.

- **Vacation limits**—During the year, most families find some time to get away. Whether it is a long vacation to a faraway place or a local day trip, these times are important for reducing stress and building memories. Typically, families of children with feeding issues struggle to have even the most basic of vacations because they cannot travel any significant distance away from the accepted feeding locations. With only so many acceptable snacks (if any) that will be eaten in different locations, the family can be limited to leaving home for only a couple of hours before needing to return to eat. So often, families report great concern for the siblings of the child with feeding issues, whose needs may be overshadowed by the restrictions imposed by the feeding disorder. These types of family-system stressors will be discussed further in the book.

- **School limits**—Families and school teams often report that they have tried for years to increase the child's feeding repertoire. They have used tokens, prizes, models, first-then procedures, social stories, rules, and reprimands but none of these have had any lasting, positive impact on the feeding disorder. Many school teams have also attempted to incorporate feeding treatments into education plans (IEPs, IFSPs). When the teams do experience success, they often then struggle with the strategies for generalizing and sustaining gains. Commonly, students are not able to fully participate in school activities because of food restrictions. They may refuse to be in situations where other students are eating unacceptable foods, or they may be overly tired due to hunger and so are less available for instruction.

Unfortunately, this limits learning and social opportunities. Further, students with feeding issues are often treated differently by adults and peers because of the behavioral challenges (e.g., screaming, tantruming) that sometimes accompany feeding issues.

- **Cyclic issues**—Virtually every event involves eating or is somehow associated with food, such as sporting events, the seasons, the school year, holidays, and annual parties. For many children, these events signal "starts" or "stops" to eating cycles and also are cues for dramatic changes in accepted and refused foods. For example, a local festival may mark the end of "summer foods" and the start of the "fall favorites," causing the entire family to adjust its eating patterns immediately. Very commonly, there are foods that are eaten only once annually at special events (e.g., bratwurst at Oktoberfest). This would not typically be a significant issue for most but for someone with feeding issues, this can mark the one and only time of the year that her feeding repertoire expands. For the families of these individuals it can be extraordinarily frustrating to watch a passing moment of tolerance in the presence of consistent and often global refusal.

- **Food availability issues**—A child that will only eat a few foods is limited by the relative availability of those foods, and the family must continually adjust to ensure they have access to those foods. Very often this means having a sizable stockpile of certain items—enough for daily consumption, to pack up and send to school and other locations, and to buy time if the local store is out of something. Often, a family's daily and weekly schedule revolve around ensuring that these foods are available, and they experience great stress when they aren't. Frequently, parents will report anxiety because they have to tell a sibling that she can't eat a particular snack because it must be saved for her brother. The internal stress on the family is quite profound and so parents will do everything possible to avoid such stressors. In extreme situations, there are so few foods that the child will eat, and they are associated with certain brands, that families will reach out to suppliers to acquire discontinued flavors, brands, or packaging.

Home Life

Not only does the whole family experience stress due to concerns over the nutritional health of the child with feeding issues, but the broader dynamic within the family system is affected. This impacts all features of daily life including scheduling family plans, school attendance, childcare, family vacations, and community participation, such as dining with other families. At home, the impact on the daily life of the family can be seen in virtually every aspect of the family's functioning. There are few routines or plans that don't need to be adjusted to accommodate the feeding limitations. For example, parents will often go to great lengths to ensure that an ample amount of a particular cracker or chicken nugget is available in the house at all times. Over time, as the family struggles to adjust to these restrictions, the long term impact of the stress caused by negotiating these difficulties can become profound. There might be interpersonal difficulties between parents, between siblings, and between parents and their children without food issues.

Family routines such as meal preparation are typically the most significantly affected. Very often families will give in and cook separate meals for their child with food restrictions in order to minimize conflict and increase the likelihood that their child will eat. Even getting used to life with these accommodating routines doesn't eliminate the stress. Siblings often grow resentful of the fact that their brother or sister always seems to get what they want when it comes to mealtimes. And maintaining a constant supply of preferred foods in the house can be frustrating, if not impossible.

In addition to the actual preparation of food, other mealtime routines are likely to be affected, for example, when and where the family eats meals and under what circumstances. Children with feeding restrictions very often feel they need to eat at the same time and in the same place every day. This can be especially challenging when trying to accommodate everyone's different schedules (i.e., afternoon soccer practice or tutoring). The child with food issues may insist on eating in the same chair or with the TV tuned to a certain show. It is not uncommon for families to report that eating a meal together is always accompanied by watching a specific program. Regardless of each family members' schedules or preferences, the entire family needs to accommodate the child with food restrictions in order to ensure that she is able to eat a full meal.

Aside from these rituals, there can be countless others associated with feeding. Children with autism spectrum disorders and food restrictions commonly develop complex routines—entire sequences of behaviors—that must be completed before mealtimes. For example, a child may need to first pick up all the toys on the playroom floor, walk through the entire house, and then sing several songs before she is ready to sit down for a meal. This can create great stress in a family when time is of the essence and constant planning for the duration of a mealtime routine is impossible. Certainly, utensils and other objects directly identified with the meal are commonly associated with rituals. For example, a child may require a specific plate, fork, cup, and placemat (each positioned perfectly) in order to tolerate eating even the most highly preferred foods.

Parents may be further restricted when it comes to food options because their child(ren) experience food intolerance or allergies or other specific dietary restrictions. For example, many children are gluten or lactose intolerant. Furthermore, parents might have to contend with the fact that one of their child's few preferred foods is only available at certain times of the year or in particular places (e.g., where they vacation). All of these challenges, when combined with the limited functional communication skills of many children with ASD, can create a painful eating experience that over time establishes a behavioral routine for food avoidance.

School

Not only does food selectivity impact the family dynamic, participation in school is also affected. Feeding limitations have a substantial impact on a child's ability to engage meaningfully in social and educational settings.

Children with food restrictions are limited in peer interactions during mealtimes within the school environment because they often choose not to eat in groups or in the cafeteria due to sensory issues, social avoidance, or their strict adherence to complex rituals. A child who will not tolerate the smells or sights of nonpreferred foods is unable to participate in a "lunch bunch," for example. For reasons such as these, feeding limitations can have a marked impact on a child's ability to participate in all school environments. With decreased food intake, overall attention and focus for academic participation may also be compromised. As a result, school teams sometimes incorporate feeding objectives within Individualized Education Programs (IEP). This is a complex task that teams often struggle with due to the challenges of developing effective feeding interventions. For many families, their child's food restrictions make the most frequent social teaching opportunities in school impossible to access. Clearly, the impact of food restrictions on the social skill development for children with ASD is complex and significant.

In addition to the social impact of food restrictions at school, it is important to consider factors associated with safety. For many children, the overall management of food is affected by oral-motor deficits, which place them at greater risk when eating in school. A busy cafeteria with loud voices and strong smells can contribute to relative behavioral dysregulation. Combined with oral-motor skill deficits, this behavioral dysregulation can interfere with the effective and safe management of food. For example, Shannon, a child who struggles with distractibility and tolerance to noise, finds it difficult to eat in her school cafeteria. Her distractibility leads her to shift her body in her chair, causing her to gag as she twists in the chair. In Shannon's case, having her eat in low distraction settings may decrease the likelihood that she will gag during a meal, but this will also exclude her from peer learning opportunities. Here, our intervention must address system-level issues that surround the feeding limitations such as motor skill development, attention, and environmental accommodations. We will discuss treatment approaches in detail in Chapter 6.

Community

Not surprisingly, the family-system issues associated with feeding limitations expand into wider community settings. Parents report that their children will not eat in restaurants or unfamiliar settings, including those that provide very familiar foods. As a result, they must adjust all family plans to allow for a consistent location for meals. Local community activities and vacations are commonly avoided by the family due to the challenges associated with food restrictions. Family gatherings are often negatively affected by the feeding difficulties experienced by the child with autism. This can include both an inability to get the child to eat anything and problem behavior that occurs when the child is in the presence of certain foods (e.g., grilled burgers, birthday cake). Until one has lived with a child with these challenges, she may not have a full appreciation for how much eating affects daily plans and the extent to which food is a central part of many activities.

Extended family and friends, while well-intentioned, often offer advice or other comments about the families' choices and methods of intervention surrounding the feeding disorder. For example, family members may attempt to encourage the parents with advice such as, "Well, if you just tell her she has to eat it, and wait her out, eventually she will comply." This type of counsel rarely considers the complex behavioral profile of a child with an autism spectrum disorder and can leave parents with feelings of resentment or doubt about their caregiving abilities. Ultimately, the feeding challenges can contribute to isolating not only the child from accessing all environments but can isolate the family as well.

3 Understanding the Basis of Feeding Challenges: Why Won't He Eat?

Joanne was frustrated. Her three-year-old daughter, Roxy, had refused yet another meal. Her pediatrician reassured her time and time again that toddlers seem to "live on air" and that she shouldn't worry. Roxy's height and weight were fine for her age and she appeared to be growing as expected. But Joanne felt that there was something more than just picky eating causing Roxy to restrict her food choices. As a baby, Roxy was so difficult to nurse that Joanne eventually put her on a bottle to get some food into her. She did eat the Stage I and II baby foods, but only a few kinds, and oddly enough, mostly only the orange ones. She refused to transition to Stage III foods and still will only eat Stage II vegetables.

Unfortunately, Roxy can't express herself very well as to why she refuses most foods. She was diagnosed at age two and a half with Pervasive Developmental Disorder: Not Otherwise Specified and her language is definitely behind that of her peers.

At this point in time, her entire repertoire of foods consists of chicken nuggets, several Stage II fruits and vegetables (carrots, sweet potatoes, apples), yogurt, milk, Cheerios, and several different kinds of chips. Joanne has tried new foods over time, but Roxy screams, cries, and even throws her food when it is not what she expects.

It has become almost impossible to include Roxy in family meals. In order to "successfully" finish a family meal, Roxy needs to be served only highly preferred foods while watching a favorite TV show on her father's smart phone. When Roxy was very little, her parents could sit her at the table and, as long as she had favorite toys to play with, she would sit for most of the meal. Now her challenging behaviors at mealtimes are so sig-

nificant that she can rarely sit for even a portion of the meal. When told to sit down, Roxy will typically arch back and fall to the floor. She will scream if picked up, and if her parents persist, she will kick and throw objects.

Joanne's friends try to persuade her to "stay strong" and not give Roxy any of her preferred foods—only new foods—to expand her repertoire. On occasion, Joanne has tried to bribe Roxy to try new foods. But every time Joanne gets up the courage to try something different she remembers the time that she tried to hide a piece of banana in Roxy's oatmeal. Now, Roxy refuses to even look at oatmeal! Her occupational therapist tried to get Roxy to put her hands in dry rice, pudding, and Play-Doh, but it took months to get her to explore these textures. Even now, Roxy will touch sticky materials with the tips of her fingers and make a very strange face.

Joanne won't admit it to her friends, but Roxy still gets a bottle of milk every night or she refuses to go to sleep. Roxy can't use a cup at other times effectively as most of the liquid spills out of her mouth. For water, Roxy uses a sippy cup, but it has to be her Dora the Explorer cup, or she won't drink. Once, when Joanne left this cup at her mother's house, Roxy wouldn't drink anything but her nighttime bottle until Joanne drove the four hours to get the cup. Now, Joanne has three spares for such an emergency.

Roxy's parents are very frustrated and have discussed the challenges but are at a loss as to how to proceed. They know that they want better for Roxy and the entire family but they're afraid any change will cause anxiety at home and risk further limits to the foods that Roxy will eat.

The family has sought help for family mealtimes from Roxy's therapists and teachers. They've focused on teaching Roxy to come to the table without complaining. They have been told that they need to make the mealtime foods highly preferred and the experience positive for Roxy, but there seems to be no way to break her from staring continuously at the video on the phone. If they remove this part of the routine, Roxy becomes extremely agitated. But with the smart phone in Roxy's hands, her parents feel that they can barely connect with her!

Motor Difficulties and Feeding

Parents of children with feeding disorders often report a long history of challenge around meals and eating. Many children may have had initial difficulty with nursing or taking a bottle. Mothers who opted to nurse may ultimately discontinue nursing because their babies would not latch efficiently or take enough milk. Difficult transitions to increasingly complex solids are also reported to be an early sign of eventual feeding disorders. Parents note the significant struggle that their children experienced progressing through the stages of baby food, perhaps resulting in a plateau at early stages. With this resistance, learned behaviors of food avoidance and escape further increase the child's challenges with food and meals. Often, parent concerns about feeding are dismissed by the pediatrician as "typical toddler behavior." Over time, these restrictions can increase into rigidities regarding food brand, color preference, and texture refusal.

One of the earliest signs of a feeding disorder can be the child's difficulty managing the bottle or latching on while nursing. Persistent difficulties with suck can be a sign of oral-motor difficulties that can later interfere with more advanced oral-motor management. The older child may also exhibit difficulty removing food from a spoon and food may spill out of the mouth frequently. He may also demonstrate difficulty chewing foods that do not break down easily in the mouth, like vegetables or meats, and may also try to move food inside of the mouth with his fingers. Food preferences may cluster around those foods that are easy to chew, including soft foods or crunchy foods that "melt" inside the mouth, like chips. He may also demonstrate difficulty transitioning from a bottle to a sippy cup or straw. While drinking, spilling may be noted and this may be particularly evident with an open cup. The child may also demonstrate difficulty with tongue and lip play skills like blowing "raspberries" or making clicks with his tongue.

Drooling is very common in infants, particularly when teething begins. For children with feeding difficulties, this drooling may persist past toddlerhood related to poor oral-motor management. The child may lack lip, tongue, and cheek control for reasons such as low muscle tone, poor coordination, or poor motor planning resulting in saliva spilling from the mouth. The parent may notice this most when the child is playing or concentrating on a particular task. If a child is unable to manage his saliva due to this poor oral-motor control, he may ultimately have difficulty managing food inside of his mouth. He may have difficulty moving food from one side of his mouth to the other (a skill essential for effective chewing). He may not be able to keep food inside of his mouth and may even chew with his mouth open. Using a cup, spoon, or straw may also be challenging due to these oral-motor inefficiencies.

Oral-motor difficulties may also been seen in association with more global motor difficulties, including overall decreased muscle tone and compromised postural stability and control. A child with an autism spectrum disorder may show difficulty maintaining an upright position for extended periods of time when he is not provided adequate trunk stability, including having his feet placed firmly on the floor or on the footrest of the highchair. Parents may find that their child slides forward in the chair, ultimately affecting his ability to have efficient head over trunk positioning. Without a sufficient postural base, the child may get tired quicker in the chair, especially if he has to work to maintain an upright position for the meal. Ultimately, he may try to get out of this seemingly uncomfortable positioning and leave the meal before it is finished. Motor difficulties can also make it difficult for the child to manage utensils well, and the child may refuse to feed himself with a spoon or fork well beyond his peers.

Signs of Motor Challenges with Feeding:

- Persistent drooling beyond toddlerhood
- Difficulty transitioning between stages of baby food
- Difficulty managing a cup or straw
- Difficulty handling utensils
- Difficulty removing food from a utensil
- Difficulty imitating such oral patterns as "raspberries"
- Sliding forward in a chair
- "Munching" patterns of chewing beyond toddlerhood
- Difficulty managing foods that require sustained chewing, like meats
- Excessive wiggling in a chair

Sensory Issues Around Food

All foods have sensory features that make them distinctive. Foods provide tactile feedback, both when they are picked up and later when placed inside of the mouth. Some children may avoid touching foods on their high chair tray or plate, and become upset with physical contact to just their hands. Parents may notice that their child doesn't put his fingers in his yogurt and spread it over the table like other infants. He may use the very tips of his fingertips when touching foods and materials that offer an unusual texture. He may show extreme reactions to having his face wiped or his teeth brushed, and may ultimately learn routines to avoid these self-care tasks. Parents may notice early on that their baby doesn't mouth toys like other babies. Sometimes, a startle reaction occurs when the baby or young child even touches a toy with an unusual tactile component. There is a correlation between decreased tactile or touch tolerance and decreased oral tactile tolerance. Very often, parents may find that their child avoids touching stringy foods and sticky materials and may even dislike walking on grass and sand for the first time.

Foods also have other distinctive sensory features. Foods have specific colors and may have bumps, ridges, or smooth surfaces. Foods also have particular smells and are usually the first introduction that the child has to a specific food, as the experience of the smell of the food generally precedes the child tasting it. For example, the strong smell of a pot roast cooking in the oven may be difficult for the child to endure. This can lead to the child avoiding the kitchen or becoming upset as the smell travels through the home. Some children will refuse to ever taste a particular food based on the smell alone.

Signs of Possible Sensory Issues with Feeding

- Gagging when food or utensil touches the lips or front of the tongue
- Gagging at sight or smell of certain foods
- Excessive dislike of tooth brushing
- Extreme displeasure with having face wiped
- Not aware of food on the face
- Overstuffing or placing too much food in the mouth
- Avoidance of touching particular foods related to their texture (e.g., slimy or sticky)
- Mouthing of objects beyond toddlerhood
- Limited mouthing of objects as a baby

Once food is inside of the mouth, the texture or sensation of the food can be perceived as unpleasant. Some children will restrict their acceptance of foods based on the way they feel inside of the mouth and may avoid foods that change in texture when they are chewed, like raw carrots. They may prevent food from making contact with their lips and instead place food directly onto the back teeth to avoid the more sensitive tongue. Gagging can occur if the utensil or spoon touches the front of the teeth or lips and can even induce vomiting. Once the child feels this unpleasant reaction to the way a food or utensil feels inside his mouth, he may avoid eating these foods in the future, or even foods that may be similar in presentation.

Many children may exhibit both underlying motor issues and sensory sensitivities that will affect their ability to tolerate and manage eating foods. It is essential that the individual needs of each child be assessed so that appropriate interventions can be selected. The assessment process is discussed more fully in Chapter 5.

Social Challenges of Eating

Early on, we begin to teach children the social rules associated with eating and, more importantly, meals. With toddlers, we begin to orient them to the social expectations of sharing meals with the family and also provide praise and corrective feedback continuously to help teach. These messages are layered onto mealtimes and other family or community moments and are rarely taught with great specificity. Unfortunately, a person with ASD is likely to struggle to understand the social nuances that are conveyed through the family about the social expectations of eating. To illustrate, a family may have a rule that during meals you sit around a table and talk and share food. They may feel that watching TV is not appropriate during meals. Their three-year-old child with autism is likely to have limited awareness of the social value of sharing the meal and may also struggle dramatically with transitions from highly preferred activities to less preferred ones. For this child, the demand to come to the table and eat, leaving behind a favorite TV show, and sit while the family shares in open-ended conversations may be daunting. This social challenge, combined with other food-related restrictions, can lead to an early history of food refusal and noncompliance with family expectations.

Food restrictions may start early on as small acts of noncompliance (e.g., grimacing and turning away from food) and over time develop into complex refusal routines that are difficult for families to tolerate. Often, the early stages of feeding challenges are a set of "typical" forms of communicating preference and being independent. However, families of children with autism spectrum disorders who have food restrictions find that these expand markedly and become anything but "typical." These refusal patterns do not subside over time and, in fact, become more deeply entrenched. Mothers and fathers learn to identify the beginning of a new refusal from its earliest signs and know, from painful experience, that pressing further will likely result in an unwinnable battle.

Parents are then faced with complex choices about which battles to fight around feeding. Often, major considerations include nutrition, the family schedule, the likelihood that the child will eat anything at all, the impact on siblings, and the overall quality of the family's life together. These many factors, paired with a child's focused motivation to avoid the demand to eat, often result in a long history of accommodating the feeding limitations, thus strengthening the challenging behavior more and more.

Family Routines that May Indicate Feeding Challenges

- Adjusting mealtimes to coordinate with TV programs
- Making sure that there is great consistency in day-to-day routines
- Cooking a special meal each night in addition to the family meal
- Avoiding presenting new foods whenever possible
- Shying away from going out to new places where you have to eat
- Isolating certain snacks for only one child to eat
- Preparing food in advance to send along with the child outside the home
- Keeping a specific set of cups, plates, and utensils for meals
- Avoiding extended trips away from home
- Stocking up on certain foods to ensure that you won't run out

---

Resulting Behavioral Challenges Around Eating

This cyclic pattern of accommodating signs of food refusal and allowing the child to escape the demand can result in a rich reinforcement pattern for behavioral challenges. For example:

Mike is a six-year-old boy diagnosed with autistic disorder who experiences substantial food selectivity. He has only a few types of food that he will eat and these have been stable since he was four years old. When pressured to try new foods or even to eat foods he likes in a different way (e.g., in the car) he becomes very agitated. For Mike, agitation manifests as screaming, crying, and flailing his arms and legs. Also, his family finds that once Mike becomes agitated, his negative mood lingers for more than forty-five minutes. So, if someone asks Mike to take a bite of a food that he doesn't know or like, Mike not only becomes agitated until the demand is removed but he also remains quite upset for a long period after eating. For this family, Mike's agitation can ruin the meal and a good portion of the day.

Over time, this family has learned that avoiding agitation and accommodating Mike's food selectivity means that Mike is more likely to have a happy day (and, in turn, so are they). They have also learned that if you take away a demand very quickly, at the first signs of agitation, Mike is less likely to have a prolonged episode. Mike's parents have become hyper-attentive to signs of agitation so that they can quickly accommodate Mike's needs and help ensure that he has a positive day. His father says, "You can almost smell the agitation in the air when it starts," as a way to describe how sensitive he is to it.

Not wanting to see their son suffer and lose the opportunity to have a positive day, the family has inadvertently provided Mike with a rich level of reinforcement for agitation. The earliest signs of this behavior now mean that something will change for him, which makes something he doesn't like go away. As Mike's parent became increasingly attentive to his signs of agitation, Mike became ever more sensitive to those things that would trigger him, and together they have reinforced each other.

By the time families seek treatment for feeding challenges, patterns such as the one Mike and his parents built are typically well established and resilient. Behavioral challenges associated with feeding can look, feel, and sound extremely different from one child to another; however, each of these is associated with the social and individual-specific variables that contribute to their development over time. Rigidities might involve using the same plate, cup, or utensil, or having a specific show on the TV. Some children will only eat vanilla yogurt of one specific brand, and will refuse different brands and presentations. Rigidities of any type are common among individuals with autism spectrum disorders and so we must consider that food-based rigidities are as prevalent as any other specific behavioral challenge. For individuals on the autism spectrum, the rigidities may be enhanced in intensity due to co-occurring complications with oral-motor functioning and sensitivity to the sensory features of food.

Whether the child refuses to eat by screaming and throwing food or by simply spitting out everything that is fed to him, the interactions between these behaviors and the social environment and family system is key. For parents and practitioners, understanding why and how these problems become established will guide treatment.

4 Proactive Strategies for Home Use: What Can We Do *Now*?

Molly's family is ready for a change. For as long as they can remember, Molly has had a narrow food repertoire, but this has always been attributed to her age. More recently, she started resisting new foods, and over time, things have gotten increasingly worse. Now, even foods that her family used to be able to convince her to eat have fallen by the wayside.

Molly, now six, was diagnosed with autistic disorder when she was three years of age. She speaks well in many respects, using phrases and single words to tell people her needs, but she struggles with letting her family and teachers know why she is resisting eating. She has always taken the same foods in her lunchbox to school: yogurt, applesauce, two slices of cheese cut into precise triangles, and Goldfish® crackers. Her favorite drink has always been grape juice mixed with water, though she will only drink it from a sippy cup.

At school, Molly's teachers have noticed that she has not been finishing her lunch, and if they do not let her eat chips as a reinforcer (reward) during instruction time, she will not eat much at all until she goes home at the end of the school day. In addition, Molly has become more resistant to going into the lunchroom with her first grade class and sometimes begins to cry as she walks into the lunchroom.

At home, Molly typically refuses her dinner. She seems hungry when she gets home from school, so her dad often gives her some of her leftover lunch, but then she won't eat her dinner. When Molly can be encouraged to eat, she has been refusing most of the foods that she had eaten when she was younger and will cry until she is given preferred foods, mostly carbohydrate-rich ones like chips and crackers.

Molly's family and her teachers know that her feeding restrictions are getting worse. They fear that they may be contributing to these patterns somehow but they're just not sure how to pinpoint the actual problem and what to do. Molly's family and her team at school work well together and feel that if they can identify the problem then they can develop a plan of action to address these challenges together.

Very often, early on, families try to address feeding problems at home with strategies suggested by friends and family members. In some cases, casual conversations with therapists and educators also produce some ideas. Most families that have come to realize that food restrictions are persisting and causing a major impact on the quality of life for their child and the family at large are willing to try *any* strategy possible to improve the situation. Frequently, there are safe-to-try approaches that can be introduced at home to address various feeding challenges. They can result in a significant benefit to the affected child and to the entire family.

This chapter will offer strategies that families can begin using today to proactively address their child's feeding difficulties. These can be helpful first steps for a family as they begin their journey toward helping their child develop a healthier relationship with food and mealtimes.

Making Mealtime a More Positive Experience

- *Offer choices*—e.g., "You can choose between eating four peas or one spoonful of mashed potato."
- *Use the first-then rule*—e.g., "First smell the squash, then you can have the pasta."
- *Clearly state expectations*—e.g., We say, "take some off," to present less of the food on the spoon
- *Make the meal process structured and predictable*—Follow consistent routines before, during, and after the meal.
- *Associate positive behavior at meals with benefits after eating*—e.g., "If you take two bites of bagel, you can pick a game to play with your brother after dinner."

Making Mealtime a More Positive Experience

Offer Choices

Choice offers us a sense of control and allows us to express our relative preferences. By building choice into meals, children have the opportunity to participate in selecting their foods. This offers them an opportunity to contribute to the decision-making process and share in meal planning. Further, they have a chance to put their choices in preference order from high to low. Choice is also a very helpful strategy for parents. When parents offer choices, they can select the items they want to be incorporated and so help guide decision-making. This gives both the parent and child a chance to benefit from the choice-making process.

How the choice-making process is approached and organized will affect whether it is successful. As a prerequisite, the child must be able to make choices during other times of the day (specifically during times when there are no expectations associated with food). If a child can't make choices independently, offering them while dealing with feeding problems may be unwise. Furthermore, it is important for parents to offer opportunities for their child to select between high and low preference items. This will allow choice making to help the family understand a child's preferences overall. Also, by periodically introducing both high and low preference foods simultaneously, the parents can build variability and interest into choice making (as

opposed to always having the choice be the lesser of two evils). For example, periodically offering a choice between two favorite dinner foods (especially just after a round of more difficult choices) can help preserve the experience of choice making as a positive one for the child.

Choice-making is something that can occur at the start of a meal and can continue at any point during the meal. Sometimes families will offer choices only at the start of the meal or when challenges emerge. This may set the child up to expect choices only after challenges begin or only at a specific time in the meal. Rather, it can be very helpful to give choices throughout the meal. This will allow the child to partici-pate continuously in choice-making, giving her more practice.

Families need to be prepared for what to do if offering choices is not immediately successful. Even though a child may do well making choices most of the time, parents will need a strategy for responding when the child refuses to make any choice. This may include clearly stating rules and expectations for the child. For example, a mother of a nine-year-old with autistic disorder and significant issues with brand-specific preferences might state to her son, "You can choose between this one or this one. If you can't choose one I will pick for you and give you that food. I'll give you forty-five seconds to make a choice." When using choice as a strategy to support improved eating, families should always endeavor to use it *before* problem behaviors emerge.

Use the First-Then Rule

Using *first-then* sequences allows your child to understand the immediate expectation as well as when she will be able to move past it and onto something more preferred. For example, "*First* eat four peas and *then* you can have crackers." Or "*First* smell the chicken and *then* you can eat the chip." This simple process allows the parent to intro-duce something highly preferred only after the child has completed something that is less highly preferred. Using this strategy, some of the sting of completing a difficult task is taken out by following it up with an easy, pleasurable one. There are several things to consider when using the first-then approach. As with most other approaches it is best to use this proactively. This means that you should present the first-then sequence early on during the meal or snack, well before any challenging behavior occurs. When this is used only after challenges begin, the adult may find herself in a position of trying to de-escalate the child's behavior and win compliance. Generally, it will be better to start from a calm moment and move forward. For many children, it will be necessary to use several first-then sequences that incorporate two preferred items as you begin to build a repertoire with this strategy. This will allow the adult to gain a history of working positively with the child by offering easy to complete instructions. Over time, the adult can then intermingle more difficult first-then expectations and build on the momentum of the child's compliance with easier sequences.

As with any other strategy, once it is introduced it is essential that the family follow the first-then rule. That is, if the child doesn't complete the "first" direction, the adult must have a plan for how to move on without allowing the child to get to the "then" reward. This might involve being prepared to remove the "then" item from the meal or for the remainder of the day, or allowing the child to have appropriate chances to say "no," (in a way that is functional and safe) in which case she doesn't have to comply with the "first" request and doesn't receive the "then" reward.

When the child's challenging behavior helps to shape the first-then contingency, there is increased risk that the challenges will intensify over time. For example, if the contingency was *"First* three slices of apple and *then* chips,"* and the child began to engage in high rates of challenging behavior such as crying and throwing items and so the rule was changed to, "Okay, *first* just one small bite of apple and *then* chips," the challenging behavior would be the primary factor shaping the rule. In this situation, the child may be better supported by choosing an alternate strategy that will maintain a positive direction and limit the impact of problem behavior, for example, using one of the other strategies described in this chapter, such as offering choices.

Clearly State Expectations

So often we assume that our expectations are clear to others, especially children. We give them a general demand such as "clean your room" or "come eat" and then assume that they will know our expectations. We then offer them a combination of praise for things going well and redirection when they deviate from our plans. Very often, the feedback about the positive is general, for example, "You are doing a great job," and the feedback about the negative is direct and clear, for example, "Don't drop your food on the ground." Whether we are dealing with feeding or any other behavior, we can help children be successful by using clearly stated expectations early on in the task and then providing them with specific praise for successful behavior.

Positively stated directions will provide the child with a clear understanding of what is expected. This means telling the child *exactly* what you want to see her do. For example, "Sit in the blue chair at the table," or "Pick which vegetable you would like, peas or carrots." This is very different from a "negative" expectation such as, "Don't yell during dinner." Whenever possible we avoid expectations that only tell the child what *not* to do. As the child starts to respond we will often encourage her along by directly labeling the behavior that she is doing well, for example, "I love that you sat right in your seat." Here we have an opportunity not only to give praise but also reinforce the expectations.

Clearly stated expectations can also be of help when the child is struggling. There are many things that caregivers can do while using the expectations to offer support. For example, a child who is only partially following directions can be "differentially" praised. This means that we give extra attention to only those behaviors that are going well and in doing so increase the child's investment in these. Sometimes parents also use this strategy by directly labeling the expectations being followed by a sibling, giving extra attention to the child who is following them and setting up a clear route for the other child to also receive praise and other rewards.

When a child is not living up to expectations, we recommend using positive language in your redirection. For example, a child who is not complying with the direction to come to the table for dinner could be provided with a clear, positive direction and perhaps, if necessary, a modeling of the expected behavior. For example, in this moment a father will likely get better results if he says, "The next thing to do is put down your action figure and walk to the table," as opposed to saying something more vague and negative like, "Stop playing and listen." Then if the child complies, the father can provide direct praise for improvement. If she doesn't comply, the father can prompt her along physically as he verbally labels the expectation, "I am going to help you by taking the toy, putting it down, and walking you to the table."

Overall, these approaches help organize our language to be very clear and directly matched with the models we provide. Using positively and clearly stated expectations is likely to be part of any intervention so it is a good idea for families to actively practice using these in all settings.

Make the Meal Process Structured and Predictable

Eating a meal is a complex event with dynamic social expectations that can be confusing for anyone to interpret. Any one of us can remember feelings of anxiety and discomfort from a time when we were invited to a meal at someone's home, a restaurant, or other new location. Generally, after a few minutes we accommodate to new social expectations and apply coping skills to manage difficult moments. In these situations we rely heavily on well generalized responses that allow us to transfer that which we have learned to do at home, now without any effort, to a new situation.

However, for individuals with autism spectrum disorders, the social expectations of a meal coupled with the complex motor tasks and sensory input can create an overwhelming demand. Social routines, conversations, outside distractors, and motor and sensory experiences can make mealtimes difficult for people with ASD who suffer from feeding restrictions and may have limitations in any one or more of these areas.

Very often a great deal of comfort can be added to mealtime by increasing the predictability of the event. In fact, structure and predictability are features of most well-crafted behavioral interventions. We can proactively offer our children support by creating as many consistent and predictable routines as possible during meals. This doesn't mean that every meal must be exactly the same but rather that we can endeavor to increase clarity and structure whenever possible. This can mean having consistent places and times for eating or following consistent family routines (e.g., waiting until everyone sits to eat, taking turns when talking, passing one food at a time around the table). In general, anything that we can do to decrease unpredicted events may allow the child with feeding issues to be a bit more successful during the meal. In doing this we can increase the number of behaviors that we consistently reward and also offer repeated practice for critical skills.

When we increase the predictability of an event we proactively offer a number of supports to a child, any number of which can ameliorate upcoming demands. Common strategies for increasing predictability include:

- offering warnings of upcoming transitions both verbally and visually;
- trying to follow consistent daily mealtime schedules;

- giving the child a complete overview of the meal by taking digital pictures of critical elements in the mealtime routine and presenting them sequentially (via a social story) before starting meals;
- providing indications of when the mealtime will end (e.g., using a visual timer, following a picture sequence);
- engaging in similar pre-meal events (e.g., free play, brief cleanup, washing hands, reviewing picture sequence, sitting).

Whenever possible, it is beneficial for the entire family to follow a set routine, rather than applying consistency for one family member only. This helps all family members to function successfully as models for each other, positions the parents to offer praise to others when they are doing well (a strategy that can shape another child's behavior), and decreases demands for managing two, three, or more mealtimes (each with their own routines and procedures).

Associate Positive Behavior at Meals with Benefits after Eating

This strategy is perhaps among the most commonly attempted by families when trying to support a child with food restrictions. In fact, it is common in any context, feeding or otherwise, with even typically developing children. The way it works is we tell our child if she does the thing we are asking of her, then afterward she will be allowed to do something she really wants to do.

This is essentially a version of the *first-then* technique described above. Most of us have used this strategy in one way or another from time to time. For example, as parents we have likely said, "*If* you are well behaved at the grocery store, *then* you can pick the show you want to watch off the DVR when we get home." During meals we often make statements such as, "*If* you try a bite of chicken, *then* you can play the Wii after dinner." The strength of this strategy, in addition to it being commonly used in homes, is that it is perfectly positioned to target positive expectations. We tell a child, *if* you do something that *I* want you to do *then* you can have access to something *you* really enjoy. This procedure allows us to organize the ways that we will reward, prompt, and model. The challenge in this strategy is its tendency to be used without appropriate motivation, and so we create an *if* that isn't worth the *then*. For example, "*If* you eat your carrots *then* you can play on the computer after dinner." Here the computer may not be motivating enough to make her want to eat the carrots (especially if the child will have other times she can play on the computer).

Using positively stated language with this strategy is essential because it tells the child exactly what is expected of her and also positions the adult to directly reward a specific and positive behavior. So, in practical terms we might say, "*If* you sit at the table during the entire meal and select one food to touch, *then*..." rather than "*If* you do not yell or throw things and don't say 'no,' *then*...." It is essential that we prepare our statements this way in order to optimize opportunities to model and reward the behavior we want to see.

When crafting the *if* part of our statement, it is important that the target behavior is reasonably within reach of the child. This means considering the current level of ability of the child and selecting goals that are attainable. This can mean that caregivers will need to adjust expectations into small and reasonable targets. For a child who refuses to be near unfamiliar foods and who rarely sits at the table with others for more than five minutes, a goal such as, "*If* you sit with all of us at dinner and taste one food, then..." would be generally unattainable. Rather we might choose, "*If* you sit with us for three minutes before dinner begins and have one bite of your preferred snack," to start with. Certainly this will not be an optimal goal for this child but it might be a "right now" goal and an opportunity for a small success on which to build.

When using this strategy to associate positive behavior with access to preferred items or activities we must be prepared to honor the rule. This means delivering the reward when success is achieved and also being prepared to withhold it if the goal is not achieved. This can be a complicated process if the child is not successful and is likely then to engage in highly challenging behavior. Finally, when considering the *then* part of your statement it is helpful to select something that is special and can be withheld for special use with the rule. This will increase its overall value and allow the child to build strong momentum toward success.

Conclusion

When using any of these strategies it is important to remember that they can be applied to multiple people simultaneously. This means that families can use them for all the children (and the parents, as well) in order to increase the ease with which they are incorporated into the family routine. Strategies such as offering positive choices, increasing the structure of the meal, associating positive behavior with reward, and crafting clear positive behavior expectations are easily applied to any person or group. Very often families find that by applying these techniques to everyone, the entire family is able to function as a model for the child with the feeding limitation, siblings feel empowered and included in positive activities within the family, and parents can increase their consistency overall.

Additionally, it doesn't hurt to be reminded that most children are more willing to try new foods when they are hungry. Asking a child to take a bite of a new food prior to a meal—particularly when a desired meal or food will be offered—is a great time to explore new food options. You may want to eliminate snacks between regular mealtimes when attempting to get your child to try a new food item. Many children are more willing to try carrots, celery, or salads when they are presented on the plate prior to the meal being served when an afternoon snack has been eliminated. Using preferred condiments such as ranch dressing or ketchup with new foods can also help to bridge foods. For example, a child who loves French fries dipped in ketchup may be more likely to try chicken nuggets dipped in ketchup as well.

Techniques to Address Oral-Motor Challenges at Home

Many children with food selectivity issues also present with underlying oral-motor challenges. These difficulties may initially be observed as spitting out various foods, gagging with more challenging food textures, and inefficient chewing patterns. Children may maintain a more open-mouthed posture while chewing or may exhibit difficulty moving food from one side of their mouths to the other. Some children fatigue quickly while chewing and refuse to eat foods that require sustained chewing, including meats. For these children, it is beneficial to explore different oral-motor strategies to assist in their exploration of new food items. Ultimately, a speech and language pathologist and/or occupational therapist evaluation will be necessary to design an individual treatment program specific to your child, but general activities can be introduced to help further refine oral-motor abilities. These might include:

- **Using whistles**—There are a variety of whistles, recorders, and flutes that will improve overall lip strength and mobility that are motivating and enjoyable for the child.

- **Using straws in different sizes**—Varying the overall height and width of the straw will allow for practice of lip control, a skill needed when excessive drooling or spilling liquid out of the mouth is evident. Additionally, having the child practice sucking thicker liquids (or even something like applesauce) through the straw can help increase lip strength.

- **Blowing bubbles**—This can also improve lip control. If blowing bubbles is too difficult, the child can blow a feather or Ping-Pong ball across a table.

- **Oral-motor imitation**—By mimicking exaggerated facial expressions (e.g., monster faces, fish faces, wide smiles, kisses) the child can improve overall motor control and in doing so help build the skills necessary for more advanced eating, such as removing food from a spoon or moving food from side to side in the mouth.

Children with underlying oral-motor challenges may initially try or taste a new food, but ultimately spit it out because of the amount of sustained effort it takes to manage the food once it is in their mouth. Practice with biting and chewing of even preferred foods can help refine overall skills. Using preferred crackers to bite from the front of the mouth and the back sides of the mouth can assist with biting and chewing. Presenting foods in a distinct rotation (side-side-front) for the child to bite and chew can ultimately promote a more sophisticated biting and chewing pattern and allow for the tongue to follow the food items in the mouth more successfully.

Techniques to Address Sensory Challenges at Home

Some children may initially refuse new foods because of the sensory qualities of the food items themselves. They may dislike the smell of the food or even the visual presentation of the food item and may refuse the food before they have even tried it. Children who demonstrate this type of overreaction to the sensory features of food may benefit from slow exposure to the food itself. For example, having a sliced banana in the middle of the table during breakfast without any request to try it will allow the child to become used to the visual presentation of the banana as well as the smell. Sliding the plate closer to the child over the course of a week will assist the child in tolerating a stronger banana smell. Eventually, the child can be prompted to slide the plate closer to her mother. Over the course of the week, as she grows more tolerant of the sight and smell, she can then be prompted to touch the banana with her index finger, and then slide the plate over to her mother. The bananas can be placed next to the plate and the child can be asked to place a banana slice on the plate, and then slide it over to her mother. With this slow exposure to the sight, smell, and touch of the food, she can be asked to pick up the banana slice and smell it and then place it on a plate. She can ultimately be prompted to place the banana to her lips, teeth, and inside of her mouth.

Use the techniques laid out in the section above, "Making Mealtime a More Positive Experience" to motivate your child to tolerate

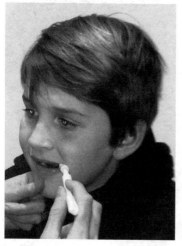

exposure to new foods. Remember that when the child resists the exposure, it will be helpful to break it down into small and smaller steps. The goal is to have the exposure be tolerable and successfully completed by the child.

While some children exhibit exaggerated avoidance responses to the sensory qualities of food, some children benefit from added sensory input. Providing heightened spice or sweetness to new foods can add desired interest to foods and ultimately improve awareness of food inside of the mouth. Use of lemon, cinnamon, garlic, and salt are all flavors that can additional interest to selected foods. Some children benefit from carbonated soft drinks prior to eating to provide increased sensory input. Providing tactile stimulation to both the outside of the mouth and inside prior to eating can also offer needed input. Using a Nuk™ brush or a toothette on a daily basis can assist with needed input to the oral structures of the mouth. These tools can be used over the lips, teeth, inside cheeks, and even tongue as tolerated. These tools can also be used prior to meals and/or tooth brushing.

Proceed with Caution

There are a number of strategies that families consider using that we feel should be thought about with great care and approached cautiously. In our experience, we've found that many of these techniques can be associated with increased challenges, ultimately impacting food acceptance and even loss of previously accepted foods. These include:

- *Hiding food*—Attempting to hide new foods under or in preferred foods can be risky. If the child finds the hidden food and pulls it out of her mouth, she may become very upset and resistant to accepting the once preferred food again. Also, if the child is unable to safely chew the hidden food, it can be a choking risk.

- *Withholding food*—Families typically find that if their child with an ASD is highly resistant to eating, "waiting her out" won't be effective. After hours of not eating or drinking, the parents begin worry that the child hasn't had any nutrition and end up offering preferred foods anyway. The result can be an unintentional teaching session for the child that refusing and waiting will ultimately lead to getting the desired food.

- *Taking a "sensory-only" or "motor-only" approach*— Interventions that globally apply sensory-motor strategies without full assessment and coordination with behavioral supports are unlikely to address the complex needs of children with ASD and feeding disorders. Some practitioners use only oral-motor strategies such as working with whistles and other motor-strengthening activities and don't introduce new foods into their interventions. Others do introduce new foods but do not establish behavioral interventions for essential skills, such as using functional communication to express needs and preferences, learning to work with clear expectations, and shaping challenging behavior into successful behavior.

- *Punishment*—When faced with trying to help a child with feeding restrictions begin to eat more foods, families and caregivers can find that applying punishment to the problem behavior (e.g., screaming and refusing) can seem like a viable option. For example, "If you scream and don't eat your chicken, you'll have no computer time." Occasionally, this may work and offers a brief alleviation from the problem behavior; however, punishment without strong teaching and reinforcement procedures generally fails to lead to lasting change. Further, when the problem behavior continues and the punishment procedure fails, the child is generally upset and has had yet another negative experience with eating and the caregiver feels disempowered.

Conclusion

This chapter provides strategies that can be used to increase interest in trying new foods and reduce food challenges in general. In many cases, these can offer meaningful improvement in individual and family quality of life. By increasing motivation and decreasing sensitivity, families can address behavioral rigidities as well as sensory-based aversions. Whenever exploring proactive supports, families should be sure to try one method at a time, move slowly, and be as consistent as possible. If more extensive intervention is necessary, the knowledge gained through trying some at-home strategies will help inform treatment planning.

5 | Community-Based Assessment of Feeding Disorders

The Friedman family has been struggling for well over a year with Luke's food restrictions. Luke is an active six-year-old boy who was diagnosed with autistic disorder at four years of age. When Luke turned four-and-a-half, the Friedmans began to notice that he strongly preferred crunchy foods and that he stopped readily trying new foods. When they tried to encourage him to eat more, he would cry and thrust backward in his chair. Now, he will gag when new foods are put into his mouth and will eventually spit them out. When told to come to the table for meals he will typically start to cry and run from the room. If his mother or father chase him, he will scream and kick away from them until they offer him chips or another crunchy food to have at the start of (and typically then throughout) his meal.

The Friedmans have tried many home interventions such as giving Luke clear rules and incentives for coming to the table. His mother purchased many new toys and offered them to him for eating, but even these highly motivating items have had little impact on Luke's feeding difficulties. The Friedmans have also tried to start meals with highly preferred foods and then sneak in something new. This has been consistently met with gagging and, in fact, causes Luke to stop eating for the remainder of the meal. His parents have tried cooking many crunchy foods, knowing that he enjoys them, hoping perhaps that this will help bridge the gap between accepted and new foods.

As the family discussed Luke's eating habits one night while cleaning up dinner they realized that all their efforts had resulted in few gains and that Luke was becoming more and more ritual-bound and restrictive.

They also realized that it had been months since they tried to introduce any new food to him and that they were changing more and more of their family patterns to accommodate Luke's rigidities. It was clear to them that it was time to consider seeking outside support for Luke and the family. They need to find a team of clinicians who can assess Luke's difficulties and provide him with treatment.

Many parents first notice feeding problems in their children with ASD during early childhood, particularly in the toddler years. At this point in time, underlying oral-motor deficits and challenging behavior patterns become more apparent and begin to greatly influence the dynamic within the family. Greater expectations are also placed on children of this age: foods become more sophisticated and closer to regular table food, and children are expected to sit for greater lengths of time at the table and engage with the family in a more structured way. Families of children with feeding restrictions often try interventions at home based on family and friend suggestions and while some ideas may prove helpful, most families end up frustrated by limited progress or, in fact, a gradual worsening of the situation. In the end, families wind up seeking assistance from community supports such as their pediatrician, school, Birth-to-Three providers, or other community practitioners such as psychologists, occupational therapists, or speech and language therapists.

Professional Intervention and the Young Child

For oral-motor challenges, parents can access several types of providers to address these areas of deficits. For children under the age of three, early intervention services, or Birth-to-Three, can be an appropriate first point of service provision. Many times, these services may already be in place as a child with ASD may demonstrate other areas of challenge, including language delays, gross and fine motor coordination deficits, and issues with social interactions and adaptive living skills.

Parents may need to explicitly explain the feeding difficulties to the providers to ensure that their child is evaluated appropriately. Some service providers use therapists as more of consultative support to the teachers and teacher assistants that work directly with the child. Children with these types of feeding difficulties must have the team's occupational and/or speech therapist directly evaluate the feeding challenges and develop a specific plan to address the identified areas of concern.

In Birth-to-Three, the team occupational therapist will evaluate the child's sensory functioning, or how the child responds to the sensory world around him, particularly considering tolerance to touch and textures. The occupational therapist will also evaluate the influence of these sensory features on the child's performance and consider ways to structure the environment to minimize sensory distractors in the home. Seating options (e.g., highchairs) will also be evaluated to ensure that they provide the necessary postural foundation while eating. The occupational therapist will also assess fine motor coordination, looking at how the child uses utensils and cups, and self-feeds. Some

occupational therapists have special training in feeding and will look at the overall feeding process, though this may instead be done by the speech and language pathologist on the team.

It will be important to find out which discipline evaluates feeding skills to ensure that the correct team member will evaluate your child. Either the speech and language pathologist or the occupational therapist will assess the overall feeding, or eating abilities. They will ask the child to drink liquids, take a bite of food from a spoon, and self-feed a favorite food. They will look at the child's chewing abilities across a variety of foods to assess any mechanical difficulties while chewing. Additionally, the speech pathologist may also look at speech production. The occupational therapist and/or speech and language pathologist may ultimately develop a plan to address any identified oral-motor challenges within the context of their service hours. Specific goals and objectives will be developed on the Individual Family Service Plan (IFSP) with designated hours assigned to these goals. For example, a child may have a goal of closing his lips firmly around a spoon to remove food.

For school-aged children, feeding intervention can again be provided by the occupational and/or speech and language pathologist. At the school level, the occupational therapist will ensure that the chair and table height is appropriate to the child for lunch and any snacks. Any risk of choking or aspiration will be noted by the nurse, occupational therapist, or speech and language pathologist and communicated to all necessary caregivers. The occupational therapist will assess self-feeding abilities and may recommend such adaptive equipment as a special cup or weighted spoon to facilitate independence. The influence of sensory distractors will also be evaluated by the occupational therapist in the classroom and lunchroom to assess how the child is able to filter out these stimuli to attend to the meal safely and effectively. The environment may need to be structured to minimize these distractors, including organized placement at the table or use of a "lunch bunch" group. For example, some children may participate in a "lunch bunch" that occurs in a small room with a few other children and a therapist structuring the time to allow for practice of feeding skills and, very often, social interaction skills. The speech and language pathologist or occupational therapist may assess the child's ability to use utensils, chew different types and textures of foods, and drink liquids in different settings that the child will typically eat. If feeding difficulties are identified by the team, specific goals and objectives will be developed for the Individualized Education Program with designated treatment hours assigned.

For some children, it may be determined that their oral-motor and behavioral needs require more specialized and time-intensive programming. These children struggle to meet the goals outlined in their educational programming and, typically, have needs that extend beyond the scope of more educationally-based interventions. The educational team may have difficulty comprehensively assessing the needs and outlining an effective treatment plan or the family may feel that the services aren't sufficient to achieve long-term gains. Services following a more traditional medical model may be recommended and accessed through a variety of different types of providers, including hospital-based occupational or speech therapy programs as well as behaviorally-based interventions. Additionally, independent or private practices may also be considered for these services. There are some practices that specialize in addressing feeding challenges via a feeding clinic model and this may be an appropriate choice for those children with autism because of their expertise in understanding the complexity of the spectrum and the many associated self-regulatory challenges.

What to Look for in a Provider

Assessment procedures typically begin during the first phone call from the family to a community provider. At this time, some general information is gathered by the community provider about the needs of the child and by the family about the practitioner and the services offered. The treatment of feeding disorders requires expertise from many areas. The family should understand the different disciplines (for example, psychologists, behavior analysts, occupational therapists, speech therapists, nurses, and nutritionists) that are part of the treatment team and how they work together to support treatment. There are several features of strong community providers that a family can look for as they research options in their area:

- A treatment team that incorporates the family in the assessment and treatment process is essential if family members are going to enable carry-over of treatment gains from the sessions to the home.
- The treatment team should support only those clinical activities that are grounded in science. This means that all interventions have clearly defined parameters with strategies for consistently measuring outcomes and adjusting procedures as necessary.
- The team should be able to complete a comprehensive assessment of feeding difficulties resulting in an understanding of why these challenges are present and what needs they are currently meeting for the child. This means that the families should expect the assessment to answer questions about their child such as: What skills does he lack to help him eat more independently? Why does he scream and run from the table when we show him new foods? What communication and coping skills does he lack that would allow him to more independently eat, share meals with the family, and communicate his needs?
- The treatment should be something that allows for a generalization plan to be completed. This means that the

family should clearly understand how the treatment team envisions transferring gains from treatment to real life settings.

Parents should seek out practitioners in their community with expertise in these areas who can support, at all times, the application of transparent evidence-based procedures. This means that the family should be able to ask of the community providers a clear description of the protocols used, the evidence that supports their application with their child, and a summary of all data collected and the decisions that the team rendered from these. At no time should a family be in a position of having to blindly trust the assessment and treatment process. In fact, clearly explained procedures that allow a family to easily understand the questions to be studied and the interventions to address limitations will be a cornerstone of appropriate evidence-based assessment and treatment procedures for people with ASD and feeding difficulties.

Community-Based Assessment of Feeding Difficulties

From a behavioral perspective, all behavior is functional. This means that any behavior, whether positive or challenging, serves a purpose for the person. Generally, behavior allows us to get at experiences, items, and sensations that we desire and avoid those we dislike or are painful for us. Typically, we think of needs for attention, delaying or escaping demands, gaining access to items or experiences, and internal stimulation. For example, a person may take an aspirin in order to escape the negative sensation of a headache. Also, we may invite our friends to join us at a restaurant to enjoy their attention and the food. For a person with feeding challenges, the various food refusal behav-

iors are also functional. For example, they can allow children to avoid demands to eat, avoid challenging motor tasks of eating foods, avoid unpleasant tastes, textures, temperatures, and smells, gain access to preferred foods, gain access to things they want, gain the attention of others, and gain access to positive sensations or avoid negative ones.

For these reasons, the process of assessing feeding restrictions relies heavily on completing a comprehensive function-based assessment of each problem behavior. This involves interviews with family members, observations, and direct assessment of the challenges with the child. Completion of this level of assessment requires support from a clinical team with expertise understanding feeding difficulties *and* autism spectrum disorders from an evidence-based applied behavior analytic (ABA) perspective.

Preparing for a Community-Based Assessment

When starting assessment there will be a process for collecting general and then highly specific information about the child and the specific feeding limitations. Assessment typically begins with collecting general information about the child and family such as diagnoses, past interventions, and the history of the present concerns. It is essential that the treatment team understand the history of the child medically and developmentally in order to clearly organize assessment questions and inform treatment choices.

A phone interview process is often the start of the intake and assessment procedure. During this time the family will speak with someone who will help gather pertinent information and also guide the family with understanding what information they should collect to share with the clinicians. This may include previous psychological assessments, feeding evaluations, occupational and physical therapy assessments, educational plans, medical records, and related evaluation and treatment documents. Before the child arrives for direct assessment of feeding difficulties, the family should participate in a comprehensive information gathering process about daily routines, foods eaten, liquids drank, behavior challenges, and family-based interventions currently underway. This will allow the family and the assessment team to study the pattern of the family's routines over a period of days and study this information to identify trends, areas of concern, and likely first points of intervention.

A family is likely to be asked to complete a food diary (see Form 5.1 on the next page). This will be a gathering of information about the child's day-to-day eating and drinking patterns. This diary should be collected over a period of days, often one full week (during a time that the child is healthy) in order to paint a picture of the week's routines. This should include patterns from the week (for example, breakfast before school, snack at school, lunch at school, snack after school, dinner, and snack before bed) and the weekend. A food diary is a very important resource to the assessment team for studying the current patterns of behavior. Furthermore, this diary can be filled out again when treatment is completed to help the family see the change over time.

The Importance of Determining High Priority Foods

As community treatment teams come to understand the needs of the child with respect to feeding and his broader profile, it will be essential that the family offer information about high priority foods to be mastered during treatment. The selection of the foods to be introduced during feeding treatment is a complicated issue and requires a great deal of ongoing attention. This must include information from the family about foods that are typically eaten at home, in school, and in the community by the family and support system for the child. When selecting the appropriate foods to initiate treatment with, the family and clinical team need to consider the immediate motor and related behavioral needs of the student and also the social context of the family.

Applied behavior analysis (ABA) requires all interventions to be based on high quality data and matched well to the life context of the individual. This means that no treatment team can unilaterally recommend foods, but rather there must be an ongoing dialogue between the family and community providers. Without this, it is likely that recommendations would be made for foods that are unlikely to be eaten at home. Which foods to introduce also requires the assessment team to identify the needs of the child and match treatment recommendations to these needs. This means that food selection requires the team to understand the family system, to functionally understand the needs of the child, and then to match these two factors together.

The beginning of the assessment process should include a way for the family to record high priority foods and submit this information to the treatment team. This will then allow the family and treatment providers to maintain attention to the family's high value foods

Form 5.1 | Food Diary

Name: _____ **Date:** _____

Date	Time	Food/Drink Consumed	Approx. Amount Consumed

Source: Feeding Clinic: Center for Children with Special Needs, Glastonbury, CT, USA

Form 5.2 | Priority Foods for Your Family

Name:_____ **Date:** _____

Please provide us with a list of foods that your family typically eats that you would like to see your child enjoy.

Breakfast: _____

_____

_____

_____

_____

Lunch: _____

_____

_____

_____

_____

Dinner: _____

_____

_____

_____

_____

Snacks: _____

_____

_____

_____

_____

Source: Feeding Clinic: Center for Children with Special Needs, Glastonbury, CT, USA

as they move forward with intervention planning. Very often family members complete a list of high priority foods, delineated by meals and snacks, that they submit as part of the assessment (see Form 5.2 on the previous page).

Video Documentation

In addition to paperwork, the family should consider providing the treatment team with videos of mealtimes and other feeding-related times at home. This can be a very complicated process for families but is of great value to treatment teams that cannot spend significant time in the home. Families often report that they have difficulty setting up the video camera at home and then capturing the footage without upsetting the already precarious dance of the mealtime routine. Though this is clearly a complication, the benefit is quite great. There are a number of critical moments that can be captured on video by the family:

- **The transition from other activities to the meal.** For example, when a father enters the playroom and announces that dinner will be served in three minutes.
- **The arrival of the child to the table.** For example, as the child is guided into the kitchen and lifted into the chair while crying and thrusting his body away from the chair.
- **The moment that food is presented to the child, including if choices are offered.** For example, when Mom puts down the plate and says, "Look! Your favorite: chicken nuggets and ketchup." Or, when Dad presents two plates and says, "Would you like chicken nuggets or spaghetti?"
- **A close-up shot of the child when taking bites of a variety of preferred foods.** Often, this includes foods that can be chewed, removed from a spoon, or drunk from a cup, for example, a handful of crackers, a bowl of applesauce, or a cup of juice that is placed in front of the child during after-school snack. This will allow the assessment team to better understand the motor or related adaptive supports needed.
- **Problem behavior that occurs when nonpreferred foods are presented.** (This is often the most difficult moment to capture as families have frequently stopped presenting difficult foods long before starting the assessment process.) For example, a grandmother takes some roasted vegetables from her plate and places them onto the plate of her grandchild.

- **The accommodations that must be made during the meal to help the child eat.** For example, a mother and father that peel the cheese off of the pizza and then remove the oregano from the sauce.
- **The end of the meal when the child is dismissed from the table or eating area.** For example, a child that is told, "Yes, you can go. Please put down your cup," before he bolts from the table and back to the playroom.

Direct Needs-Based Behavioral Assessment

Once all of this background information is collected, the child is ready for direct assessment. This will be a process of working with the child and the family to complete specific observations of the child's needs. Typically, this will begin with an interview completed with a primary caregiver before the child is presented with any direct assessment tasks. The interview process allows the parent to review the information that was submitted to the team and talk through the assessment tasks. This marks an essential part of the process for building a strong relationship between the community providers and the family. If the family members are unclear about the assessment tasks to be completed, it is likely that they will experience great anxiety and feel disconnected with the assessment process. The best implementation of evidence-based assessment procedures utilizing applied behavior analysis as a treatment guide will require that the family clearly understands and is supportive of the assessment process.

Community-based assessment procedures will often offer the family opportunities to participate directly in the assessment process. This can include providing the parents opportunities to serve as co-therapists during the assessment and to give the clinicians direct feedback about how the assessment procedure is or is not aligning with "normal" day-to-day experiences. For example, the mother of a five-year-old boy arrives for assessment at an outpatient feeding clinic. She has completed the intake information and provided substantial information about her child's history. As the direct observation and assessment begins, she watches in amazement as her son eats every food item given to him. She comments that the foods he is accepting during the feeding assessment are among the most difficult ones to get him to eat at home. The psychologist working with them, building on these comments and all the information that has been provided about this boy before the assessment, is able to ask the mother to work directly with the boy in the treatment room. Then, as the child begins to resist the foods given by the mother, the therapist immediately returns to sit with the mother as she offers the foods. The resistance given to the mother then transfers directly to the therapist during the session. By allowing the mother to both understand the assessment tasks and participate directly in the assessment, the therapist is able to achieve a clear picture of the challenges faced at home and also learn a great deal about the variations in the child's behavior based upon factors such as who he has eaten with before, or where he has been given food.

The direct feeding assessment of the child requires that various environmental features be presented systematically so that observations can be conducted of the child's behavior. This allows for a comprehensive "needs" assessment to be completed that specifically addresses the skill deficits and related instructional *needs* of the child. In taking a needs-based perspective, the direct assessment of feeding difficulties considers not only why problem behaviors are occurring but also what skills are absent that would allow the child to be a successful eater in the future. The goal of identifying what skills to teach should guide any assessment of feeding difficulties. From this, teams may also identify problems, determine their causes, and develop interventions to minimize them.

When direct assessments of feeding challenges are conducted, it is essential that the complete scope of possible needs of the child be completely investigated. This will allow assumptions to be avoided that are not sufficiently complete or representative of the child's needs. For example, based on the general information provided from a family, a clinician may assume that a child refuses to eat most foods because he wants to avoid eating "new" foods. After an appropriate direct assessment we may find that the child refuses to eat most foods because the sensation of complex textures is aversive to him and, further, when he refuses food, he is typically incentivized to "try" with favorite TV shows and desserts. This offers a more extensive conceptualization of the child's needs and therefore better directs appropriate treatment.

Assessment procedures will expose the child to various conditions that help systematically evaluate the function of behavior. In doing so, the assessment will aim to determine those conditions that reliably evoke challenges and those that do not. When this level of systematic control can be achieved, the treatment team is very well positioned to design highly successful interventions. To complete this task, it will be important that the family and clinical team are comfortable with the process of exposing the child to various conditions that may trigger challenges. While this, for a short time during assessment, may trigger problem behavior, it is typically worth the investigation in order to map the specific variables that are most directly associated with the child-specific feeding needs. Such conditions are likely to adjust the levels of demand, attention, and preferred items presented to the child in relation to the presence of nonpreferred foods.

Direct Oral-Motor Assessment of Feeding Difficulties

During an oral-motor assessment the therapist will obtain an early feeding history, including how the child nursed or used a bottle, how the child transitioned to solid foods and between stages of foods, and a history of respiratory infections. This history of respiratory infections can indicate inefficient swallowing and the provider may ultimately recommend a swallow study to ensure safe and efficient swallowing. A history of gagging or vomiting should also be obtained and evaluated to determine the influences of contributing sensory deficits on eating over time.

The occupational therapist on the feeding team will also assess your child's general postural stability and control and its effect on his ability to maintain an adequate base while eating. The therapist will assess generalized muscle tone and any compensatory strategies that your child uses, such as sliding forward in the chair and wrapping his legs around the legs of the chair for added stability. Overall fatigue and activity tolerance will also be assessed to ensure that your child is able to stay seated for an entire meal.

General sensory processing abilities will also be analyzed in relation to meals and eating. Every environmental setting offers different kinds of sensory influences, whether it be bright vs. faint lighting, the hum of a refrigerator, or other children in the family clamoring for dinner. Some children with ASD have difficulty filtering out sensory distractors around them and may "over attend" to unimportant or irrelevant sensory triggers, like the air conditioning starting up, while missing important, salient features like their mother requesting they eat another bite of food.

In the therapy setting, the therapist will assess auditory sensory processing, tactile or touch sensitivity, visual distractibility, olfactory (smell) tolerance, and taste tolerance. The clinician may work with the family to establish a procedure for measuring these environmental features day-to-day so that they can be compared against the child's

behavioral profile. The therapist is looking to understand any underlying sensitivities that may affect the child's success with eating. The therapist may also look at balance reactions, particularly in relation to maintaining balance in a chair and proprioceptive functioning, or body-in-space awareness. Proprioceptive functioning will also let the child know how much force to exert on a utensil or how much food to place in his mouth. For a feeding assessment, sensory processing abilities will be directly measured in relation to the environment during feeding as well as the overall features of the food itself in the context of oral-motor management.

The Taste, Texture, Temperature Inventory (Powers, 2008) is a Likert Scale instrument that can be used to quantifiably measure the child's overall tolerance to food items based on their quality (see Form 5.3 on pages 72-73). Foods are analyzed for their spiciness, texture, and temperature and the child's overall acceptance is referenced for each of these specific food measures to better establish a profile of foods that the child will eat. This will allow the therapist to begin to determine patterns of foods that the child prefers or avoids. Many children with autism spectrum disorders with feeding difficulties dislike foods that are mixed in texture or lumpy. Some children avoid foods that require sustained chewing or drinks that are carbonated. The Taste, Texture, Temperature Inventory allows the therapist to track improved tolerance to food types over time as well—an important consideration for progress measurement. This tool will also assist the clinician in choosing appropriate foods with which to start intervention since food choices can be matched against the food types that are most commonly accepted by taste, texture, and temperature.

Form 5.3 | Taste, Texture, Temperature Inventory

Name:_____ **Date:** _____

Inventory completed by: _____

Please circle the number that best corresponds to each statement.

Strongly Prefers	Prefers	Tolerates	Dislikes	Strongly Dislikes
5	4	3	2	1

1. In relation to salty foods, my child:

5	4	3	2	1

2. In relation to sweet foods, my child:

5	4	3	2	1

3. In relation to foods that have an unusual texture, my child:

5	4	3	2	1

4. In relation to foods that are mushy, my child:

5	4	3	2	1

5. In relation to foods that are crunchy, my child:

5	4	3	2	1

6. In relation to foods that are chewy, my child:

5	4	3	2	1

7. In relation to foods that are cold, my child:

5	4	3	2	1

8. In relation to foods that are sour, my child:

5	4	3	2	1

9. In relation to foods that are hot, my child:

5	4	3	2	1

10. In relation to foods that are spicy, my child:

5	4	3	2	1

11. In relation to foods/drinks that are carbonated, my child:

5	4	3	2	1

12. In relation to foods that are mixed in texture, my child:

5	4	3	2	1

13. In relation to foods that are lumpy, my child:

5	4	3	2	1

Please list some of your child's favorite foods: _____

_____

_____

_____

Does your child ever gag at the smell of certain foods? Yes/No? Which?

_____

_____

_____

Does your child ever gag at the sight of certain foods? Yes/No? Which?

_____

_____

_____

Does your child dislike having his/her teeth brushed? Yes/No? Explain:

_____

_____

Does your child regularly take vitamins? Yes/No? Which?

_____

_____

Additional Comments/Information: _____

_____

_____

_____

_____

Source: Feeding Clinic: Center for Children with Special Needs, Glastonbury, CT, USA

Another important component of the oral-motor evaluation is oral-facial observations. This allows the clinician to assess any facial asymmetry or alignment deficits. Dental issues can also be addressed, such as evidence of bite misalignment or actual missing teeth, a common observation in young children. This information is important in treatment planning as missing front teeth or molars can affect which types of foods are chosen for intervention as well as where foods should be placed inside of the mouth.

Just as general muscle tone provides the foundation for an adequate postural base, oral muscle tone provides the foundation for the mechanical abilities of feeding. For many children with autism spectrum disorders, decreased muscle tone may be evident. Decreased oral muscle tone can lead to inefficient oral-motor patterns for lip, cheek, and tongue control. Some children may stabilize their jaw by keeping it firmly in place, which limits the development of an effective way to chew. Often, children may use their jaw to guide how their tongue moves. This can drastically impact how these children move food inside of their mouths. The clinician will evaluate for the influence of muscle tone deficits while eating and any compensatory patterns that are observed as well. Additionally, overall endurance while eating may be affected by muscle tone deficits and this will be evaluated during the assessment process as well.

For some children with ASD, the persistence of latent oral reflexes interferes with eating. We are born with certain oral reflexes that help us survive as infants, including the gag reflex and the bite reflex. In most cases, oral reflexes are well integrated by eight months of age. However, with some children, these reflexes can persist and adversely affect eating skills. Commonly, community providers working with children with autism and feeding difficulties report a persistent gag reflex interfering with overall food tolerance. Most of us will gag when food or dental implements trigger the back third of the tongue. This experience is noted by most of us who have ever had a strep test swab. However, for some children with feeding difficulties, they may exhibit a hyperresponsive gag reflex with stimulation to *any* part of the tongue. Some children demonstrate a gag response to just the visual presentation or smell of a particular food item. Another reflex that may be assessed is a bite reflex, or a spontaneous bite with presentation of a spoon or other utensil. The assessment of persistent oral-motor reflexes is critical to the development of an effective treatment plan.

The clinician will begin to expand his overview of the structures of the mouth while feeding. Jaw control will be assessed with presentation of food. The clinician will examine how much the child opens his mouth in preparation for a bite and how much he opens his mouth while chewing; some children exaggerate their jaw movements while chewing, demonstrating poor jaw control.

Lip control will also be assessed: The clinician may prompt the child to imitate lip pursing or retraction and observe his ability to close his mouth on the bowl of the spoon or on a straw. Additionally, observations of food or drink spilling out of the mouth while eating or drinking may indicate decreased lip control as well. The clinician will also assess cheek musculature while eating. He may ask the child to puff out his cheeks to blow or observe how the muscles work while sucking on liquids or chewing.

Tongue movements will provide another important observation while eating. The clinician may ask the child to perform a tongue "wag" by imitating a pattern of moving his tongue from one side of the mouth to the other. Tongue lateralization allows the child to move food from one side of his mouth to the other and this should be carefully observed during the assessment. Occasionally, low muscle tone causes the child to use compensatory movements to help move food inside of the mouth. A child may demonstrate an immature pattern of control by moving the food forward in and out of his mouth instead of moving it from side to side with his tongue by pressing it downward in his mouth, or holding his jaw firmly in place to provide stability while managing food. Observations of tongue movements will also show any preference for one side of the mouth or the other. At times, a child may stabilize on one side of the body—and mouth—to provide himself with additional stability and ultimately control. For example, we may see him hold his body upright in the seat with his right arm to add support. Over time, these patterns can become habitual and difficult to adjust.

As the underlying mechanical skills to feeding are evaluated, the clinician will also examine feeding behavior and subsequent feeding skills. The examiner will assess the child's ability to prepare for a bite of food. When presenting a bite of food to a child or adult, the mouth opens in preparation for taking the food into the mouth. For those children with autism spectrum disorders and feeding challenges, this oral planning may not occur and may even result in resistance when the food approaches the mouth. When the food or utensil enters the mouth, the child may not spontaneously place his lips around the food and begin to chew or move the food inside of his mouth. The clinician will need to closely examine these skills that prompt effective food management.

Once the food is inside of the mouth, overall chewing abilities will need to be evaluated. By two to three years of age, rotary chewing patterns become more refined and allows food to move in a circular pattern from one side of the mouth to the other while chewing. For many children with ASD, this rotary chewing pattern is compromised resulting in less mature "munching" patterns, in which the food is chewed in a up and down pattern. The clinician will also assess the child's ability to swallow a portion of food while continuing to control

the rest of the food in his mouth, a skill that is refined up to age three. Overall endurance while chewing will also be evaluated. Liquid management will also be assessed (including bottle control when appropriate) as well as more advanced liquid control with use of a straw, sippy cup, or open cup. Spilling with both liquids and solids will be observed.

Independence while eating will also be examined across a variety of foods and liquids. Self-feeding skills with finger foods like crackers and chips will be compared to skills with utensils, including a spoon and fork. The child's ability to place the spoon in a bowl with foods that may stick to the spoon, such as yogurt or pudding, and scooping such foods as cereal and pasta will be assessed. Additionally, the child's ability to use a fork, involving placing the fork in the food, spearing the food, and ultimately moving the food into his mouth will be noted. Higher level skills, such as using a napkin to wipe a messy face will be examined. The overall tolerance to food left on the face, will also be evaluated.

The following are some questions that parents of children with ASD will likely be asked during a feeding assessment. As part of the assessment process, clinicians will want to determine:

- Can the child maintain lip closure on the bowl of a spoon?
- Can the child move food from one side of the mouth to the other while eating?
- Does the child gag when foods are placed on the tongue?
- Can the child efficiently remove food from the utensil?

Answers to these questions are determined through parent interview and the actual oral-motor assessment. Understanding where the child's challenges are helps guide decision making for treatment priorities. These answers will also assist the clinicians in determining foods that the child will be able to successfully manage at the start of treatment. Further, the information will help guide decision making about the best ways to start presenting new foods. For example, if a child cannot move food from one side of his mouth to the other with his tongue, treatment should not begin with a complex food, such as chicken breast, since this requires a lot of chewing before swallowing.

6 | A Family-Centered Approach to Treatment: What Should We Expect?

Andrew is an eight-year-old boy with autistic disorder. He has struggled with a great deal of ritualized behavior, language delays, and limitations in play skills. Additionally, he is delayed with most aspects of feeding. Since he was four years old, his mother, Irene, and father, Bob, have had almost no success with introducing new foods except for bland carbohydrates, such as plain bagels and crunchy snack foods. Andrew will eat some foods reliably. At this time these include French fries, plain bagels, Lays® potato chips, hot dog buns, Goldfish crackers, and pizza without cheese or any visible spices in the sauce. He will also eat purple colored yogurt that is blueberry flavored and without lumps of fruit.

At times, Andrew will drool when he is concentrating hard on a given activity (for example, while playing on the computer). His family has also noticed that as he eats he pockets food in his cheeks. This is often most noticeable with foods like the hot dog buns and bagels. Occasionally, his parents need to help him to clear his mouth and have done so by encouraging him to drink or even by swiping their fingers into his mouth.

When Andrew eats, he follows a complex set of rituals that frequently shift. This makes things particularly complicated for his family because they often find that once they have accommodated for one ritual, a change occurs. When this happens, Andrew becomes very agitated and refuses to eat, and then the family begins their investigation of what the new ritual needs to be. Over time, these rituals have evolved from particular places to sit while eating, to different plates that are okay to eat off of, to toys that need to be at the table, to statements that people can or cannot make during meals (for example, his father can say "Way to go," but not "Good trying"), to TV shows that need to be on or off during meals.

Over the past year, Andrew's parents have noticed that their daughter, Gloria, has been observing Andrew and copying some of his challenging behavior. She has thrown food, demanded favorite plates, refused to eat the family meal, and has raised questions such as, "Why do I have to eat this if Andrew gets to eat something special?" This has made the parents very concerned about not only Andrew's progress but the impact of his food restrictions on the overall family dynamic.

Irene and Bob have tried a number of "at-home" strategies to help Andrew. They created a family incentive system wherein the kids would earn stars toward privileges after dinner. They found that Gloria excelled with this and would push herself to eat new things but Andrew showed no interest in the stars or his family's praise. Bob developed a video model of one of Andrew's cousins eating a meal in hopes that Andrew, who has strong preference for this cousin, would want to "be like him." Again, Andrew showed no interest.

After this, his mother and father decided that they would set clear expectations and a First-Then rule (e.g., "First take a bite of the meatball, then you may watch TV"). Occasionally, Andrew would take a bite using this technique but the results were not consistent. On most nights they would fight with Andrew, trying to make him take the bite and avoid watching TV; however, after an hour of so they found that they had far less fight in them than Andrew had and the demand would be removed. Faced with the rest of the evening and limited free time activities that Andrew can complete independently, he would inevitably end up watching TV anyway.

Andrew's family has worked with his school team and some community practitioners to address concerns with behavioral rigidities and language delays. The community supports have included outpatient occupational therapy and speech therapy. The OT suggested using very spicy foods to heighten his awareness. He also suggested hiding nonpreferred foods under favorite foods on a spoon. To help with "regulating" his arousal, the therapist recommended using a brushing protocol using a surgical scrub brush on Andrew's body several times during the day. His mother followed through with treatment for over a year but did not see much change in Andrew's behavior, including his feeding.

The speech treatment included many activities to strengthen Andrew's mouth muscles. The SLP worked with him using whistles, chewing tubes, straws, and gummy foods. In speech treatment, Andrew was often *very compliant with direction but did not show substantial gains at home, school, or in the community.*

The school team also attempted to improve Andrew's eating habits. They provided him with rules for eating during snack and lunch times. For example, "First bite this carrot, then you can have a chicken nugget." These practices led to extremely disruptive behavior and a refusal to eat during lunch or snack.

By this point, Irene and Bob decided that Andrew required a comprehensive feeding intervention that would help him stop refusing previously accepted foods and finally make some progress toward eating a healthy diet. Irene enrolled Andrew in a community-based feeding clinic and, following a comprehensive assessment, he began weekly treatment.

Once the assessment process has been completed, direct treatment can begin. It is essential that the treatment procedures be driven specifically from the assessment data so that all interventions can be closely monitored for their impact on the child. This includes all interventions to address motor, sensory, and behavior challenges.

During treatment, interventions will proceed sequentially. This means that skills will be ordered to allow for a meaningful progression that is both achievable and rewarding for the child. At all times, family members should be able to ask treatment providers to describe the current interventions, the reason for their selection, current status, and expected impact on the child's progress. Asking such questions from time to time will allow parents to better understand the current status of treatment and to evaluate if their child is making meaningful progress.

Identifying and Teaching Prerequisite Skills

Many preparatory activities are used at the beginning of treatment. These can include oral and general behavioral strategies. The goal is to establish the prerequisite skills of eating and sharing in a meal. It is important that the treatment team consider not just that the child should accept more foods but that these should be accepted in the context of a meal. This means that families should be prepared for a feeding intervention that spends a good portion of the beginning of treatment addressing skills that *seem* to be directly associated with eating more foods.

In order to even begin the process of introducing new foods, there are several behaviors that need to be mastered, and it is appropriate for a feeding intervention to address these prerequisite skills to ensure successful mastery of food introduction. This should include skills necessary for participating in direct teaching of new behaviors as well as those necessary for sharing a meal.

One of the most common examples of such skills is sitting safely at a table and being able to receive direction. For many children this prerequisite can require great attention at the start of treatment with many different behavior support strategies applied in order to achieve mastery of this core skill. Mastery of this ability is critical as it opens the door for all future instruction. For some children, this can mean that feeding treatment begins with very specific directions for skills that lead up to appropriate sitting. For example, a child might spend the majority of the initial portion of feeding treatment playing with toys on the floor and eating preferred foods; however, she must take all preferred toys from a table top. Then the toys might be placed on the table and the child is expected to sit at a chair at the table for one moment before taking them. After this, the child might be asked to eat a bite of a favorite food before taking the toy to play. Eventually, she arrives at sitting for longer and longer periods and working on more complicated demands before she may return to the carpet to play. The time spent on this, seemingly nonfood-related skills, is absolutely essential for success in feeding.

There are several other essential prerequisites that must be addressed such as accepting directions, voicing interests, making appropriate refusals, and following basic rules and expectations. Family members should expect that successful interventions will address all of the behaviors associated with feeding. Without this component of treatment, a child is highly unlikely to make lasting gains. Again, an appropriate perspective on feeding treatment will address much more than simply accepting new foods. The person must be able to stably accept foods and explore new ones while sharing a social mealtime experience.

With this goal in mind, families and feeding teams can more comfortably appreciate the scope of the intervention required. This further underscores the importance of the feeding team working in close collaboration with the family so that realistic expectations are set for treatment and so that these match well with those likely to exist in the person's daily life. Feeding treatment will take a shared intervention approach where time is dedicated to behavioral challenges directly associated with food acceptance and also the social repertories that wrap around meals. This perspective toward treatment allows families the opportunity to greatly expand the skills that are considered appropriate for treatment, ensures that the feeding team takes a socially meaningful approach toward intervention, and that the child has many skills that are feeding-related and can be richly rewarded but not require trying new foods. This helps to build positive momentum in treatment where the child finds that many of the expectations set for her are achievable quickly and do not evoke anxieties associated with tasting new foods. Here, a balance is struck in treatment that positions both child and family for long term success.

Functional Communication Skills

As we consider these prerequisites, it is important to consider that functional communication skills will likely be part of any comprehensive feeding intervention. That is, it is highly likely that the family and feeding team will be helping the child to use functional communication skills to voice preferences and interests as well as to make appropriate refusals. It is essential that the feeding team be able to work with other providers (for example, community speech therapists) to appropriately coordinate training.

Communication challenges for many children with autism spectrum disorder are extensive, and specialized treatment plans are often developed to address deficits. These can include procedures for appropriately modeling vocal language as well as the use of assistive devices and related supports such as picture-based systems and digital communication devices. Families should feel comfortable asking that the feeding team coordinate training targets with other providers so that there is consistency across all communication training. Without this coordination, the child could be working on one strategy with one team (for example, handing over a card that indicates a need for a break) and a related strategy with another (for example, pushing a button on a device that then says, "Can we do this later?") without the benefit for a coordinated intervention approach that would maximize practice opportunities and expand skill generalization.

Furthermore, it is likely that a great deal of information from previous interventions could be shared with the feeding team to help improve the efficiency of intervention. The key message here is that the treatment of feeding challenges will likely involve functional communication training to help the child more independently navigate her world. This means that the feeding team must be prepared to work with others to help collaborate interventions to ensure consistency and the most efficient and effective treatment possible.

Building Tolerance for Oral Stimulation

The community-based team will ask the family to bring their child in to therapy with the feeding team. At that time, they may begin to familiarize the child with the various tools that will be used during intervention. The Nuk brush may be used to provide oral-motor input and may later be used as a tool to support the introduction of new foods. The Nuk brush is a tool that is used by occupational therapists and speech and language pathologists to provide oral-motor stimulation and work on desensitization to texture or tactile stimulation within the mouth. The brush has a nubby, flexible tip that can hold small pieces of food in its folds. There are other commercially available tools that offer rounded, smooth tips and tools that vibrate.

At first, the child may only tolerate stimulation to the outside of her mouth, beginning with her cheeks, chin, and to the outside of her lips. With familiarity, the child may even open her mouth for continued exploration to her front teeth, inside of her lips, and to her back teeth. Stimulation applied to the front or back of the tongue may result in a gagging response, so the therapist may slowly introduce the Nuk brush to this area.

The therapist may use specific verbal cues paired with the introduction of the tool in order to establish a positive relationship with the demand and the tool. The tool can be placed to each side of the mouth and to the front teeth or lips in a predictable pattern. Using a phrase such as "side-side-front" will also let the child know exactly where the oral implement will be placed and when the oral-motor intervention will stop—an important cue when oral input may be less tolerated. Some children may understand "one-two-three–all done" more readily and this can be used instead as the verbal prompt to assist with predictability. Some children may be less tolerant of the Nuk brush or other tool used to stimulate their tongue and lips and initial intervention may be aimed at touching the teeth if this is more easily tolerated.

Success here then builds a bridge to tolerating other stimulation.

Once the child tolerates stimulation to the inside of the mouth with an implement such as the Nuk, the therapist may explore other utensils designed to provide oral-motor input. Another device that the therapist may use is a textured spoon. This is a spoon that has ridges on the outside bottom of the bowl of the spoon. This can provide for a transition between tools such as a Nuk and a standard spoon. With the introduction of these oral-motor tools, the feeding team may also begin to introduce other tools as well. Whistles, available in many styles and levels of resistance, allow for continued desensitization to the lip area as well as improve lip strength and overall lip control. Prompts may be provided by the therapist to stabilize the child's jaw to encourage lip movements separate from the jaw.

As tolerance improves, stimulation can be provided to the front and sides of the tongue as well as the lips. Preferred foods and liquids can also be placed on the Nuk to begin to address food management along with the oral-motor skill development. Foods such as pudding, yogurt, and Nutella® stick easily on the oral-motor devices and are often foods that are tolerated by children. Placing foods to each side of the mouth in succession will encourage

the child to lateralize the tongue, or bring the tongue from one side of the mouth to the other—an important skill for food management. The Nuk brush or other tool can be placed in the front of the mouth and drawn out slowly to prompt lip pursing around the tip of the instrument. The child's wiping of the food off of the lips after this task may be an indication of hypersensitivity within the lip area. Continued emphasis may be placed on lip desensitization if this is observed and the team may need to consider introducing foods to places other than the lips, such as the teeth. The therapist may even work on approaching the lips by desensitizing the child to touch near the lips but on the exterior of the mouth.

Many children with feeding challenges prefer crunchy foods that "melt" once inside the mouth and that do not require sustained chewing efforts. Consequently, many children lack the ability to chew for longer periods and may even spit out those foods that require more effort, like meats. Often, the feeding team will choose foods that will stick on the Nuk or other feeding tool as the beginning target foods. These foods are typically pureed or smooth in texture as they offer little oral-motor effort to manage them as well. No chewing is involved and by using a small amount of the food on the tool minimal tongue movement is required while still allowing the child to slowly get used to the taste of the chosen food.

Developing Chewing Skills

As the feeding team begins to progress with beginning oral-motor intervention, homework may be assigned. Parents may be asked to practice improving their child's tolerance to the Nuk or other implements alone or paired with a preferred food or liquid using a designated verbal prompt to promote familiarity. The team may also begin to address improving chewing skills using foods that are already preferred. Foods such as bagels that have been left out on the counter to make them chewier may be recommended. Fruit roll-ups, thick toast, licorice ropes, and gummy bears all require sustained chewing effort. The team may also suggest that the child practice biting preferred foods with her front teeth as otherwise she may "stuff" food into her mouth instead of using her teeth to bite off a small amount. Again, preferred foods can be used, though the parent may have to hold the food in her hand as the child bites the food.

These skills can be demonstrated during therapy so the parents can feel comfortable practicing them at home.

Seating Position

During intervention, the feeding team will have the child sit in a chair with her feet flat on the floor and her hips and knees positioned at ninety degrees. A small stool or box may be placed under the feet if the child cannot reach the floor. It is very important to consider seating during any feeding intervention, including where the child will sit at home. Some children may exhibit low muscle tone and therefore have difficulty remaining in an upright position for an entire meal. She may rest her head on her hand or slide forward onto her sacrum while eating.

For effective swallowing, the child should have her head positioned over her trunk for the entire meal. The therapist may recommend a piece of nonskid matting, or Dycem, be used to prevent the child's bottom from sliding forward in the chair both during therapy and at home. The child may also need a stool or box placed under her feet, particularly if a standard kitchen or dining room chair is used for meals. Parents may want to consider using a child's table and chair set for practicing feeding skills at home. The feeding team will also recommend that the school team evaluate seating for lunch and snack at school as well.

Generalization

All skills taught in a community-based feeding clinic must be generalized to the home. This process will begin with the prerequisite skills and move forward progressively to more complex feeding behaviors. In order to achieve this, family members must be welcomed into treatment. This means discussing the process of treatment, observing it, and eventually directly participating in its implementation. Often, families will find that they are not included directly in the treatment process and so implementation at home is a difficult and unclear venture. At all time, family members should be comfortable asking treatment teams to give them a plan for how they will be directly trained on feeding interventions. This should give families a sense of when they will work as part of the community-based treatment team to guide the process of implementing treatment. Just as assessment is essential to guide treatment development, caregiver participation in the treatment process is essential to skill generalization. That means that parents should expect that they will directly participate within sessions and also be charged with at-home implementation of practice activities.

Home Practice

All functional community-based feeding interventions will rely on a strong home collaboration process. Typically, this will include a procedure for setting up home practice sessions that are run daily. This allows the child to experience treatment that moves systematically from in-session therapy to home practice. As stated above, this process begins with practice on all feeding prerequisites. This allows family members to set up a procedure for home practice before introducing complex new feeding skills. In doing so, the family prepares the child for the first steps of working with new foods in the same fashion as does the outpatient treatment team. This parallel process is another hallmark of highly impactful feeding treatments.

When preparing for home practice, families will typically set up special ways to work on feeding that are different from other things the child does at home. Families benefit greatly from identifying a specific area and time of day for starting home-based generalization of feeding interventions. Again, this process may start with practice on core prerequisites before the family introduces new foods. When running practice sessions at home, families must be prepared to work on specific skills that were targeted during outpatient treatment. This can include generalization of motor and other behavioral targets associated with food acceptance and will systematically expand to include more complex feeding skills such as eating new foods and sharing in meals.

Very often parents will set up a schedule for the day that includes something like "Tasting Time." This indicates for the child the specific moment when she will practice doing those skills she worked on while at the community-based feeding treatment center. In order to set up such home practice sessions, families may need to organize a designated area for working on feeding skills. Typically, this includes a child-sized table and chair that are separate from any place that the child currently eats. Occasionally, families wonder about why this differentiation is encouraged. Given the behavioral rigidities often experienced by children with autism *and* feeding disorders, it can be highly therapeutic to initially separate practice with feeding skills from areas where the child currently eats some foods (whether at a table or on a couch). This can help prevent the child from associating potentially negative feelings about feeding skills practice with the foods that she currently eats.

Families may worry that by increasing the home demands associated with feeding that the child will lose any foods that she is currently eating. By providing an alternative setting, the child can be given a practice setting that is clearly distinct from any meal or snack areas. Also, by creating a predictable schedule, the child is better able to understand when certain demands will be made and when they will be withheld. This also protects from creating a home environment that is nebulous and full of inconsistent feeding demands. To illustrate:

Andrew has now been enrolled in feeding treatment for several weeks and he is starting to show some gains with early feeding skills. For example, he is starting to follow demands to sit at a table and smell new foods. He is willing to listen to small but difficult demands and attempts to complete them without extensive protesting. Together, the therapist and his mother are offering Andrew praise and time playing fun games during breaks from these demands. Andrew's mother has been attending the Feeding Clinic with her son and has worked with the team on using some of the strategies with him.

At this time, they have decided that Andrew should begin daily home practice. A small table has been placed at the far corner of the family's dining room where Andrew is expected to do his feeding practice. At the request of the feeding team, Andrew's parents have prepared a visual schedule with pictures of the bus, a change of clothing, Andrew's toys, the Tasting Time table, the yard, and the bathroom. This schedule is intended to guide Andrew through the process of coming home from school to the Tasting Time and through several other typical afternoon activities.

Andrew's mother reviewed the schedule with him several times and then carried the entire schedule around the house to the various locations and pointed out the picture on the schedule and the matching picture in the various settings. Andrew, a child who benefits from visual supports, was able to understand this progress most easily when the schedule coordinated directly with images in the specific areas.

When it was time for his first Tasting Time at home, Andrew was guided over to the table and given a puzzle to complete with his mother. Together they worked on the puzzle and then she asked him to smell three foods. After the puzzle and three quick smells, he completed his time at the table and was given a special Tasting Time reward to carry to the playroom. The goal for the initial Tasting Time had been met: Andrew followed the schedule, sat at the table, completed a simple task with no behavioral challenges, and was richly reinforced for his efforts. From here, his mother built the foundation for daily practice with feeding.

This process was then progressively expanded (though not too quickly) to move Andrew forward with more advanced practice of feeding skills. His mother's role was to guide Andrew through Tasting Time practice at home once or twice each day so that he always logged some time at the table. The activities for the Tasting Time were decided upon each week at Feeding Clinic so that everyone was always coordinated about the appropriate next steps. Typically, as Andrew mastered something at the clinic, his family was then asked to work on it at home. This helped with the generalization of skills and allowed his family to make sure the gains seen in treatment were carried over to the home environment. Furthermore, Andrew's time in feeding therapy was much better spent when he had practiced his skills each day and his family could report on his progress. This allowed the team to note challenges with generalization early on and remediate these with changes to *treatment or with expanded training for his family members on how to apply interventions at home.*

Over time, Andrew's Tasting Times expanded to include practice with oral-motor skills and tasting new foods. His family recorded information on his progress and this was reviewed at the start of each treatment session. As Andrew gained more skills in Feeding Clinic and during Tasting Time, his family and treatment team were able to make decisions about the next steps for generalization. For him, this included moving certain skills from Tasting Time to snacks and meals at school and at home.

Introducing New Foods

Once a child has mastered all feeding prerequisites, she may begin the process of exploring new foods and building the skills necessary for consistently eating them. By this time, the child should be accustomed to working with various implements such as a Nuk, straws, and any other utensils selected for use based upon her needs. Additionally, the child would have mastered prerequisite skills for participating in direct teaching for feeding such as sitting at a table, following basic directions, and working with progressions such as *first-then*. This opens the door to introducing new foods.

New foods should be identified through a collaborative decision-making process between the family and the treatment team. They must consider those foods that are a high priority for the family and those that are nutritionally indicated for the child. The assessment process, as was discussed previously, should initiate this dialogue. Throughout the course of treatment, decisions should be made based upon the child's current competencies, the family's needs, and the nutritional impact of different foods. Often times, foods that require minimal tongue mobility or other complex oral-motor management are the more appropriate to select at the start of treatment. These can include foods such as pudding, yogurt, and applesauce.

The process of introducing new foods should follow a progression that is systematic and allows the child to experience gains without undergoing great distress. This means that the treatment team must be able to:

1. adjust (i.e., break down) the consistency and texture of certain foods,
2. vary how the food is presented (e.g., smelling versus tasting),
3. change the implement or utensil by which it is presented, and
4. control the amount of food presented.

By isolating these factors and using the Feeding Hierarchy Record Sheet (see Form 6.1) the team can move forward with working systematically on the various features of different foods without difficulty.

The Feeding Clinic Hierarchy

The Feeding Hierarchy Record Sheet is a tool used by feeding teams to guide the process of introducing new foods (see Form 6.1). It provides the team with a measurable way to examine the different features of foods themselves, offers means of introduction that will allow for systematic presentation of foods, and functions as a guide to increase the complexity and the amount of food over time. When considering the different qualities of foods, teams need to be prepared to address features such as food texture. Foods themselves offer a variety of textures that require different oral-motor competencies. Pureed foods offer a consistent consistency without lumps, and typically require less oral-motor effort to manage. Ground foods are ones that are chopped into fine bits and require more sustained effort than pureed foods, but less chewing than a whole food that has not been cut. Foods of a mixed texture require the mouth to work harder as it separates the different foods using the tongue to guide firmer foods to the teeth to begin chewing while initiating a swallow with foods that are more readily managed. For children with less oral-motor proficiency, management of mixed textured foods is extremely difficult and many children avoid them due to the work that they require. Additionally, foods that appear lumpy or bumpy may be visually unappealing and subsequently avoided.

The Feeding Hierarchy Record Sheet, used by feeding teams, presents a series of texture modifications to define the consistency of the food presented to the child. For example, a child may initially only eat smooth yogurt without any chunks of fruit in it; thus the yogurt most closely matches the texture modification of the smooth presentation of food. Once the child accepts the yogurt with the fruit in it, the yogurt texture will be in its natural form. A steamed carrot may initially be modified to a ground texture, then progressed forward to a chopped texture until it is ultimately tolerated in its natural form of a whole steamed carrot.

All foods should be initially presented in their natural form to see if the child will accept that texture. Depending on the child, foods can be modified for their texture in two different ways. Some children can be presented with the texture modifications backwards from the natural form, often called "stepping back." For example, if the child refuses the targeted food in its natural form, it can be stepped back and tried in a chopped presentation. If the targeted food is refused again, it can be stepped back to the ground presentation. The food is ultimately modified in texture until it reaches the lowest texture form, the smooth presentation, and the trials will begin at this level of modification.

This "stepping back" of textures of each targeted food requires that the child have some level of flexibility to manage the reintroduction of each food in a different texture presentation. However, some children may demonstrate higher levels of rigidity in their behavior and will exhibit much more resistance with the food presented in this manner. For children with less flexibility, it may be more beneficial to present the food initially in its most modified form of texture and work up, or "step forward," as the stage of texture modification is mastered. This will allow the child to build upon positive acceptance for food introduction. This type of presentation for texture modification may also be helpful in the beginning stages of feeding intervention when the child is only just beginning to understand the expectations of the feeding clinic.

The Feeding Hierarchy Record Sheet also defines *how* the food is presented to the child. Foods can be presented to the child in four different ways. The child can smell the targeted food. The child can "kiss" the targeted food or have the food placed on her lips. The child can have the food placed in her mouth by the adult. Finally, the child can self-feed the targeted food. The child can be presented with a targeted food in its natural form and, if refused, modified in texture as tolerated. The feeding team can then decide if this is a child who requires the presentation style that is "stepped back" progressively or if the team should fall back to the least invasive presentation format, or smelling, and step forward as tolerated.

Usually, a food's texture is held constant while its presentation is moved forward to full acceptance of the food in the mouth. For

Form 6.1 | Feeding Hierarchy Record Sheet

Patient: _____   **Date:** _____

Directions: Use a single row per food. Summarize the day's data to represent the final level of acceptance achieved during the session. Circle the word that best represents the texture, presentation, amount, and implement used. Be sure to record any relevant comments for consistency.

Food	Texture Modification	Presentation	Amount	Implement	Notes
New: Y/N Mastered: Y/N	Smooth Ground Chopped Natural	Smell Lips Teeth Mouth Self-feed Supported Independent	Dab <1/8 t <1/4 t <1/2 t >1 t	Nuk Textured Spoon Spoon/Fork Fingers Other:____	

Food	Texture Modification	Presentation	Amount	Implement	Notes
New: Y/N Mastered: Y/N	Smooth Ground Chopped Natural	Smell Lips Teeth Mouth Self-feed Supported Independent	Dab <1/8 t <1/4 t <1/2 t >1 t	Nuk Textured Spoon Spoon/Fork Fingers Other:____	

Food	Texture Modification	Presentation	Amount	Implement	Notes
	Smooth Ground Chopped Natural	Smell Lips Teeth Mouth Self-feed Supported Independent	Dab <1/8 t <1/4 t <1/2 t >1 t	Nuk Textured Spoon Spoon/Fork Fingers Other:_____	
New: Y/N Mastered: Y/N					

Food	Texture Modification	Presentation	Amount	Implement	Notes
	Smooth Ground Chopped Natural	Smell Lips Teeth Mouth Self-feed Supported Independent	Dab <1/8 t <1/4 t <1/2 t >1 t	Nuk Textured Spoon Spoon/Fork Fingers Other:_____	
New: Y/N Mastered: Y/N					

Source: Feeding Clinic: Center for Children with Special Needs, Glastonbury, CT, USA

example, a child is presented with mashed potatoes with a smooth consistency on a spoon and asked to take a bite. She refuses and the team then "steps back" to the therapist presenting just the spoon to her. She again refuses. The mashed potatoes are again presented, though this time she is asked to "kiss" them on the spoon. This time she follows the demand and the team identifies the starting point for intervention.

The Feeding Hierarchy Record Sheet also addresses the *type of implement* that is used to introduce the targeted food. Already, the child has become familiar with various oral-motor tools, such as the Nuk brush, during the beginning stages of intervention. These tools are then used as part of the process for fading in more natural implements, such as a fork or spoon. One important factor that teams should consider is that by establishing familiarity with an implement, such as the Nuk brush, the child is less likely to struggle with tolerating the new texture of the foods. The implement will always "feel" the same in the mouth and so it helps reduce the demand associated with tasting a new food.

As with the other features of the hierarchy, the targeted food will be presented in its natural form, such as yogurt on a spoon or bagel in the hand. If the food is refused in its natural presentation, the process of "stepping back" is initiated, most typically with use of the Nuk or other preferred implement, such as a textured spoon. For example, the feeding team and the family select pasta for a targeted food. The pasta (in this case, pastina with a small amount of butter) is initially presented on a spoon along with the direction, "Take a bite." The child pushes the spoon away and refuses to take a bite. After a different preferred food is sampled, the pasta is again presented, but this time with a modification. A single piece of pasta was pushed into the Nuk brush, and the child, being already familiar with the Nuk as an oral-motor tool, allowed the pasta into her mouth and accepted the small amount of the pasta with this presentation.

The final feature of the Feeding Hierarchy that is often faded systematically is the overall *quantity* of food, or how much food is offered to the child for each presentation. Quantity is increased slowly within each step of the other features of the Hierarchy. This means that the child practices with each step of the Hierarchy at increasing quantities before other features, such as texture or the implement used, are changed. Teams need to organize their measurement of food quantities systematically so that strong data-based decision-making can inform when to step forward with more advanced presentations. The Feeding Hierarchy Record Sheet defines accepted foods in measurements of a dab, less than one quarter teaspoon, less than one half teaspoon, less than one teaspoon, and more than one teaspoon. To illustrate:

Using the Feeding Hierarchy Record Sheet, Andrew's feeding team systematically introduced a number of foods to him that were later generalized to home. For example, the family wanted Andrew to eat a food that offers more protein, as this has been lacking in his current diet. The feeding team and his parents wanted a food that could be combined with the bagel that he already eats. His school allows peanut butter in the lunchroom, so the family and the team felt that this would be an appropriate choice.

Initially, a teaspoon of smooth peanut butter was spread on a bagel and presented to Andrew with the direction, "Take a bite." Andrew refused the bagel by picking it up and throwing it. The team prompted Andrew to state, "Not now. Later." While he was being verbally prompted, the bagel was put back on the table, giving no attention to the throwing. After he complied with the demand to say, "Not now, later," the bagel was visually removed. Andrew was praised by the team, including his mother, for using appropriate language.

After several other easier foods were presented, the peanut butter was reintroduced. This time, the feeding team stepped back their presentation of the peanut butter. As the peanut butter was already smooth, no modifications to the texture were required. The peanut butter was put on the Nuk brush and the quantity was stepped back to less than ¼ teaspoon. Andrew was first asked to smell the peanut butter on the Nuk. Throughout the rest of that session, he successfully smelled the peanut butter and the team stepped forward to asking him to "kiss" the peanut butter on the Nuk. The team assigned homework for Andrew to practice smelling the peanut butter on the Nuk for the rest of the week.

At his next session, after successfully completing his homework, the team reintroduced kissing the peanut butter on the Nuk. Throughout the session, the team continued to step forward on the Hierarchy. Andrew allowed the Nuk into his mouth and removed the ¼ teaspoon of peanut butter with his teeth and lips. This set the stage for stepping forward to increased quantities as well as progressing from the Nuk to the spoon.

The Importance of Data Collection During Treatment

All evidence-based interventions require comprehensive data collection that allows for decisions to be made based upon objective evidence. This is true for the assessment process, as was discussed previously, as well as for treatment. Treatment data should be collected during each session in order to allow the team to measure gains and execute data analysis based upon the learner's performance. This data analysis process will establish the foundation for guiding, in an individualized fashion, decision making for upcoming treatment strategies.

Generally, family members should expect that every intervention component will be associated with a clearly defined data collection strategy. This means that as new foods are introduced, parents should be able to ask about the team's progress on that specific target, session to session. Further, if new intervention methods are introduced (e.g., a strategy for teaching a child to make choices among two low preference foods), these should be guided by evidence regarding the child's gains.

Feeding treatments are very comprehensive procedures and so we should expect that there will be many different layers of information collected during each phase of treatment. For example, a team may collect information on the child's challenging behavior while seated at the table, acceptance of five different new foods, use of functional communication strategies, and ability to successfully form her lips around a straw and suck up a liquid without spilling. Families should be comfortable asking teams to describe their data collection methods (always using friendly terms) and to review these with them continuously.

When new strategies are introduced to the family for use with the child, it is always important the family feel comfortable asking a few direct questions that should illustrate if the intervention is clear, evidence-based, and evaluable. Clinicians should anticipate these questions and answer them proactively whenever possible. Generally, these questions will be: What is the procedure for this intervention? What is the intervention designed to do? What will you be measuring? How will we know if it is working? What are the next steps if this works? What are the next steps if it doesn't work?

How Does Data Analysis Inform Treatment?

Data collection during the treatment session should be summarized consistently. This should include graphic analysis of the data by the team. Teams collect information on all demands placed on the child and then summarize these data into overviews of the child's progress, session to session. Over time, the feeding team and family should expect to see marked improvements in a number of areas such as the quality and quantity of new foods accepted by the child, stable gains over time, use of increasingly sophisticated utensils, improved social eating behavior, and independent functional communication skills.

It is important that the data collected during the feeding sessions are comprehensive enough to allow for strong decision making. Usually this involves direct data collection on feeding trials across a number of domains. This can include the quantity of food presented, the utensil used, modifications to the food's texture, the level of acceptance expected (for example smelling, kissing, or self-feeding), and whether or not the food was accepted in a reasonable period. Analysis of acceptance patterns by these variables empowers a team to make detail-driven decisions about a child's behavior. This leads to future decisions that are highly informed and more likely to set the child up for success. For example, by evaluating differences between acceptance rates when the food is presented lumpy or smooth on a spoon, the team may be able to understand important information about the child's current sensitivities with respect to food texture. Form 6.2 is an example of a data sheet that teams may use during treatment to collect data on food acceptance and oral-motor capabilities.

Generalizing Treatment Methods to the Home Environment

As treatment moves forward, families should be prepared to participate directly in the process of generalizing those feeding skills that have been mastered during treatment. During the initial feeding sessions, families will observe the presentation of the targeted food

Form 6.2 | Feeding Clinic Data Sheet

Patient: _____ **Date:** _____

Directions: *Use a single row per food. Circle the word that best represents the implement, amount, and level of presentation. Circle + or − based upon acceptance or refusal as long as the presentation format is stable. For Self-feed, circle S for supported or I for independent. As any presentation feature changes, use a new row for the data.*

Food	Implement	Amount	Level	Accept (<5s)	Accept (<15s)	Comments
	Nuk	Dab	Smell	+ −	+ −	
	Spoon/Fork	<1/8 t	Lips	+ −	+ −	
	Fingers	<1/4 t	Teeth	+ −	+ −	
	Other:_____	<1/2 t	Mouth	+ −	+ −	
		>1 t	Self-feed (S / I)	+ −	+ −	

Food	Implement	Amount	Level	Accept (<5s)	Accept (<15s)	Comments
	Nuk	Dab	Smell	+ −	+ −	
	Spoon/Fork	<1/8 t	Lips	+ −	+ −	
	Fingers	<1/4 t	Teeth	+ −	+ −	
	Other:_____	<1/2 t	Mouth	+ −	+ −	
		>1 t	Self-feed (S / I)	+ −	+ −	

Food	Implement	Amount	Level	Accept (<5s)		Accept (<15s)		Comments
	Nuk	Dab	Smell	+ −	+ −	+ −	+ −	
	Spoon/Fork	<1/8 t	Lips	+ −	+ −	+ −	+ −	
	Fingers	<1/4 t	Teeth	+ −	+ −	+ −	+ −	
	Other:_____	<1/2 t	Mouth	+ −	+ −	+ −	+ −	
		>1 t	Self-feed (S / I)	+ −	+ −	+ −	+ −	

Food	Implement	Amount	Level	Accept (<5s)		Accept (<15s)		Comments
	Nuk	Dab	Smell	+ −	+ −	+ −	+ −	
	Spoon/Fork	<1/8 t	Lips	+ −	+ −	+ −	+ −	
	Fingers	<1/4 t	Teeth	+ −	+ −	+ −	+ −	
	Other:_____	<1/2 t	Mouth	+ −	+ −	+ −	+ −	
		>1 t	Self-feed (S / I)	+ −	+ −	+ −	+ −	

Source: Feeding Clinic: Center for Children with Special Needs, Glastonbury, CT, USA

items, most typically four to five foods to allow for preferences and taste aversions. Families will observe the team's interaction with their child and begin to implement the treatment strategies during the session itself—a way to bridge tasting time during therapy and tasting time at home.

During these sessions, families will practice food introduction via smelling, Nuk presentation, and introduction on a utensil, based on the child's most successful skill acquisition during therapy. As with therapy, all of the foods may be presented in various modalities so the family must feel comfortable presenting foods for their child to smell, on a Nuk to their lips, and on a Nuk inside their mouth. In a home program, a child may be asked to smell one food, kiss two different foods on a Nuk, taste a small amount of a third food on the Nuk, and independently self-feed a fourth. Using data sheets will help the family organize this information more successfully as well as provide the treatment team a way to track the child's acceptance patterns each week.

Home Data Collection

Establishing a home data collection process must be a priority for the team in order to ensure that gains can be systematically followed across environments. Any home data collection process must be adjusted to fit the family's needs. It is critical that the team develop a format that works easily in the home. Most commonly, the data collection procedures will give the family clear indications of the targets to be worked on, including the style and quantity of presentation, and a very easy way to record progress. It is essential that this be done consistently so that the family gains a great deal of practice with using the data collection process.

Over time, the family will be able to suggest changes to the data collection process that will make its use in the home more successful. Typically, data collection forms that allow the family to track individual foods, day-to-day, are helpful because they organize the process for the family into a consistent set of practice trails (see Form 6.3 for a sample and Form 6.4 for a blank version). The family can easily use symbols such as + and – to indicate whether the child has accepted (+) or refused (–) the food. Also, there should be a place that the family writes notes about any unexpected events, such as large gains or unexpected challenges.

From the beginning of treatment, the feeding team should establish clear expectations with the family for the type of practice that can be achieved at home and the data that can be collected. This expectation should be discussed with a clear understanding that without a process for collecting objective data at home, the feeding treatment is unlikely to be able to ensure the level of gains necessary for long-term health.

Moving Toward Independent Eating

As the child becomes more proficient with eating new foods, the team will prompt independence with eating these foods, and indeed, a food will only be considered mastered once the child is able to feed herself these foods. Many children that begin feeding intervention don't eat foods that require utensils and so their abilities with these implements are often poor. Early in treatment, the therapist may try a scoop dish (which has a low front and high back) that helps when scooping up the food from the bowl. The therapist will typically use a smaller spoon that is appropriate to the age of the child to make it easier to remove the food once inside her mouth; it will also be easier for the child to hold as well. An offset spoon angled to the side to help position the food towards the mouth may be used if the child has difficulty getting the spoon towards her mouth. A weighted spoon may be used if the child has mild hand tremors as the weight itself will help stabilize the utensil from the bowl to the mouth. A textured spoon has "bumps" on the bottom of the spoon and can help transition the child from the Nuk to the spoon. Once the child demonstrates control with the spoon, a fork will also be introduced.

Form 6.3 | SAMPLE Feeding Clinic Home Data Sheet

Name: _Jack_   **Week of:** _12/1 - 12/7_

Food	Implement	Placement	Amount	Notes
Strawberry yogurt	Nuk	In mouth	Dab	Tell him, "1...2...3."

Best Food	Implement	Placement	Amount	Notes
Strawberry yogurt	Nuk	In mouth	1/4 teaspoon	

Day 1	+ – – + – + + +			
Day 2	– + + – + – – +			
Day 3	+ + + + – – – + +			
Day 4	+ + + + + + + +			
Day 5	+ + + + + – – + +			
Day 6	+ + + + + + + +			

Food	Implement	Placement	Amount	Notes
Chocolate pudding	spoon	front part of mouth	1/4 teaspoon	Remind him to clear the spoon.

Best Food	Implement	Placement	Amount	Notes
Chocolate pudding	spoon	front part of mouth	dab	Didn't like it and refused to clear the spoon.

Day 1	+ - - + + - - + +
Day 2	+ - - + + +
Day 3	+ - - - + +
Day 4	- + - - + + +
Day 5	+ - - + + +
Day 6	+ + + - - - + + +

	Food	Implement	Placement	Amount	Notes
	Rice cracker	n/a	front teeth	whole cracker; small bites	Present the entire cracker and say, "Take a bite."

	Food	Implement	Placement	Amount	Notes
Best	Rice cracker	n/a	front teeth	small nibbles	Liked the cracker!

Day 1	+ - - - + +
Day 2	+ + - - + +
Day 3	- + - - + +
Day 4	+ - - + + +
Day 5	- - + + + +
Day 6	+ - - + + + +

Source: Feeding Clinic: Center for Children with Special Needs, Glastonbury, CT, USA

Form 6.4 | Feeding Clinic Home Data Sheet

Name: _____   Week of: _____

	Food	Implement	Placement	Amount	Notes
Best	Food	Implement	Placement	Amount	Notes
Day 1					
Day 2			Day 3		
			Day 4		Day 5
					Day 6

	Food	Implement	Placement	Amount	Notes
Best	Food	Implement	Placement	Amount	Notes
Day 1					
Day 2			Day 3		
			Day 4		Day 5
					Day 6

Source: Feeding Clinic: Center for Children with Special Needs, Glastonbury, CT, USA

Many children with feeding challenges exhibit difficulty transitioning from their familiar bottle or sippy cup to other drinking options. Some children benefit from having the top of their bottle removed so that they have to drink out of it like a cup. Some children may transition from a bottle to a sippy cup with a spout, as it is similar to the nipple of the bottle. The child may benefit from a toddler training cup without a spout as she transitions to an open cup. Removing the rubber stopper inside will allow the child to begin to regulate the flow of the liquid.

The team will use straw work to advance the child to other methods of drinking as well as a way to improve lip pursing and lip control. A juice box or pouch may be introduced initially, as the therapist can squeeze the box or pouch to control the amount of liquid that the child gets in her mouth. With subsequent practice, the child will gain more control and begin to learn to suck through the straw more effectively. The child can transition to other straws as well once competency has been achieved. Large straws will allow greater amounts of liquid with less effort. Smaller, narrower straws require increased lip pursing and sustained control. Thicker liquids, like milkshakes or even applesauce, can be used to work on a stronger suck and sustained lip and cheek control.

Conclusion

Clearly, feeding intervention is a comprehensive process that integrates an understanding of the child's underlying oral-motor capabilities as well as the behavioral rigidities that contribute to food selectivity. Treatment for feeding challenges also needs to promote a specific set of mealtime expectations, including effective communication, an understanding of basic commands, and the ability to come and remain at the table for a meal. Data collection will help define the child's progress towards mastery of new foods and highlight areas requiring continued emphasis or modified intervention. The family is an integral part of the feeding team and will assist in establishing priority food choices as well integrating the feeding team's interventions at home for more consistent and fluent carryover of skills across different environments.

7 Integrating Treatment at Home and in the Community:
Will We Ever Go Out to Eat Again?

Maddie, a nine-year-old girl with ASD, has been progressing well in her feeding treatment. Her father and mother are feeling very hopeful about her ability to be a healthy eater. Maddie has been attending an outpatient feeding clinic for about fifteen months with her father on a weekly basis. Over the course of treatment she has begun eating over thirty new foods. At the start of treatment, Maddie was highly resistant to the sights or smells of nonpreferred foods, and would gag when presented with these. Maddie's oral-motor skills were extremely immature for her age. Additionally, she tended to be rule-governed in all of her behavior. With feeding, this meant that she preferred to eat at certain times and in specific locations. Also, only her father and mother could give her food to eat.

These challenges have emerged over the course of several years and her parents have seen progressive skill loss and an increase in rigidity throughout this period. During treatment, Maddie's therapists at the community feeding clinic addressed each of these issues with skill practice. They systematically introduced new foods based on their texture, sight, and smell, and selected foods that were appropriate for Maddie, given her oral-motor skills. Further, her family worked with the therapists to address related adaptive skill needs, such as working flexibly with change, tolerating directions from others, and generalizing skills.

The family has been running daily practice sessions with Maddie at home and she is now completing these easily. Over the course of the past six months, her family has been able to introduce some new foods *at home during practice sessions. Her parents were able to do this by working directly with the feeding therapists during the treatment sessions and then replicating certain activities at home. To achieve this, Maddie's father sat in on treatment sessions and also worked directly with Maddie. The family was given recommendations for how to construct practice sessions at home and ways to collect information on her daily progress. Additionally, they have helped Maddie eat breakfast and dinner at the kitchen table with the family, though she continues to eat only highly preferred items there.*

Maddie's parents have asked the school to start generalizing her newly gained foods to snack and lunch but their success has been limited. So far, they have been able to help her eat familiar foods at different tables and at different times but she continues to refuse new items, even though she will eat them in therapy and at home.

At this time, Maddie's family is very concerned that while Maddie is making wonderful gains during feeding treatment and in the practice sessions at home, her progress in real life settings is far weaker. Despite their repeated efforts, Maddie continues to refuse new foods at the family table and at school even though she accepts them at the feeding clinic. Her family and the feeding clinic team are now preparing to review her treatment and consider priorities. For example, should they continue to introduce new foods in the clinic, should they focus all their attention on generalizing skills, or should they attend to both of these issues simultaneously?

The generalization of the gains made in a clinical treatment setting to the home, school, and community is absolutely one of the primary challenges of any feeding treatment. Frequently, while progress can be achieved in one setting, often using complex behavioral strategies, the gains are not stable and have limited carryover. This can create a great deal of frustration for the patient and the family. Typically, family members will try to generalize foods that are now accepted at the treatment center to the home only to find that the child continues to refuse them. Frustrated by this disconnect, family members may push forward with presenting foods, but with continual refusal, the family comes to feel pessimistic about the possibility of change.

Caregiver Participation in Treatment

Any outpatient treatment of feeding disorders should explicitly plan for caregiver participation in the sessions. This is essential if the family members are to feel empowered to practice skills outside of treatment and to provide honest feedback to the clinicians about supports that are likely to be successful in the home and community. In this regard, the family will function as the bridge between the treatment of the feeding disorder in the clinic and outside the clinic. This is, of course, a primary role for family in any treatment; however, with respect to feeding, the need for direct training and consultation with the family is critical.

In preparing for engaging the family in practice sessions, the treatment team must establish a process for transitioning the family into the sessions and for giving them very specific tasks to complete at home. Daily home practice sessions allow for the treatment to have a consistent impact and prepare the child for the process of generalizing skills. Such home-based activities should be associated with an easy process for the family to collect information on gains and to report on challenges. Once home practice sessions are established and there is evidence of gains in treatment in these structured home settings, the family and treatment team can begin the process of supporting comprehensive and stable generalization of skills.

Generalizing to Home

As the generalization process moves forward, it will be important that the family work with the treatment team to select appropriate first foods to expand upon. Typically, this means beginning by reviewing the foods that have been mastered in treatment and that are strongly preferred by the child. Over the course of treatment, it is important to monitor the child's preferences, especially as many new foods are introduced. As the child gains skills and can more successfully explore new foods, it will be possible to gain a more sophisticated appreciation for characteristics of foods that are more highly preferred. This understanding should, over time, guide the selection of new feeding targets. To achieve this, the treatment team should have ongoing dialogue with the family to review those foods that are important to the daily functioning of the home and then coordinate selection of feeding targets with an awareness of the child's needs. This process requires the clinicians to allocate time for the family to contribute directly to treatment decision making and to have clear conversations about food choices that have the highest probability of success.

Once a stable process has been developed for monitoring the child's preferences and guiding the selection of new foods to introduce during treatment, it is possible to move forward with making decisions about generalization. The first step in this process is to identify the initial environment for generalization. Typically, this means reviewing the family's schedule and finding a time in the day that coordinates best with embedding a practice activity. There are a number of factors that will impact the selection of settings for generalization. These include factors such as the family's schedule, the availability of direct support and attention for the child, the importance of the setting to the family, and the child's current abilities.

When selecting an environment, parents should report to the clinicians on the family's routine. This will highlight times during the day when meals and snacks occur that are typical. Using this set of times, the team should consider the moments that are most likely to be successful for the child and the family. This will mean identifying the times that fit best with the resources needed to embed feeding practice. For example, a snack time following the child's return from school may be a good choice for one family because of the time between snack and dinner, the likelihood that the child will be hungry, and the opportunity to have a TV program on or other preferred activity happening during the snack. For another family, however, the snack time might be a matter of minutes before various sports and other after school activities begin when spending time embedding a feeding practice activity will likely be unsuccessful. To make appropriate choices we must consider time when the family is likely to be eating, when new foods that the child likes can be easily prepared, when an adult can make time available to directly focus on the feeding practice, and when the demands of the feeding are most likely to match the child's current abilities (for example, sitting on a couch to eat a snack versus sitting at the kitchen table to eat a meal).

The foods selected to use during generalization practice should be mastered in introductory phases during structured treatment. They should be of high preference to the child and make sense for the family.

As a child begins to gain foods during treatment, the family will gain a sense of those foods that are easiest for the child and that are most enjoyed. In most cases, these become some of the first foods that the family attempts to generalize. For example, if bread and American cheese have been acquired during treatment and practiced at home during structured tasting times, it may be identified to be given to the child as a snack after school. Over time, the family and feeding clinicians should establish a process for moving foods across environments and monitoring their success.

Factors That Limit Generalization

In the course of generalizing foods, it may be necessary for the feeding treatment team to address related skill delays such as difficulty coping with change, intrusive rituals, poor attention to directions, noncompliance, or problems working with distractors. Often, family members describe these issues as factors limiting generalization. While they are not food-specific issues, a feeding treatment may address them in order to help the child achieve meaningful gains.

As the generalization process moves forward it will also be important for the feeding treatment team to maintain conversations with the family about the supports put in place throughout treatment to help with the introduction of new foods. When considering the most productive strategies for supporting the acquisition of feeding it will be important that family members and clinicians consider the procedures that were most helpful with the initial acquisition of skills, as referencing these will likely help bridge generalization barriers. In many cases, the proactive supports that were discussed in previous chapters that support acquisition of new skills will be the same that help enable the generalization process. If token economies or other supports were in place, they should be considered for use during all stages of generalization. Often, these may have been faded as the child gained independence with the acceptance of new foods during structured treatment. By reviewing all the supports that were necessary during structured treatment, the team may be better equipped to support generalization. For example, a child who required use of a token board to help guide his progress through teaching trials during the initial phases of treatment might require that board to be introduced again during the generalization process.

Modifying the Natural Environment

As comprehensive efforts to support generalization begin, it will be important to consider adaptations to the natural environment that must be completed in order to ensure success. For some individuals, the tasks of working with foods across settings will go smoothly as long as appropriate foods have been selected. In other cases, however, it is necessary to consider modifications to the environment that will be therapeutic. There are several strategies that can be helpful in this regard:

- **Increase the structure of the environment**—Settings where skills will be generalized can be modified to include visual supports and other layers of structure to help the child move forward with generalization. Such levels of structure can allow the child to understand the expectations and how to identify the beginning, middle, and end of the activity.

- **Isolate a reward**—High value incentives can be layered into the environment so that the introduction of the feeding demand is less aversive. Whenever possible, this reward can be shared with multiple family members (i.e., siblings) in order to promote a sense of shared positive behavioral expectations.

- **Adjust the level of the demand**—When beginning the generalization process, as with all other phases of feeding treatment, it may be necessary to fall back to easier levels of presentation so that the child can be immediately successful. Success completing a demand and a positive sense achievement is essential when families begin with expanding generalization. Often, the family and feeding clinicians decide to "start small." This may mean that when a food is introduced in the next generalization setting the expectations are stepped down to something simple, such as smelling, before the demand to eat is introduced. For the family, they can follow a consistent hierarchy and step progressively toward stable acceptance of foods in a naturalistic context.

- **Provide models**—A sibling or other peer model can be used to help generalize foods across settings. It may be possible to first introduce the model within the structured feeding sessions and then embed the model in the generalization setting. For example, a child may come to the feeding clinic for a period of three weeks with his brother. Together they will follow a "snack plan" and each receive a reward. During this period the brother is trained to encourage the child to eat the target foods and complete the plan collaboratively. After the training sessions, the "snack plan" may be run at home.

- *Practice*—It is important to practice the generalization process. This can mean that the child will first be guided through structured practice sessions where the steps of generalization are reviewed before the target generalization food is introduced. For example, a mother may prepare a visual schedule of the evening with "Dinner" highlighted. For a period of a few days, during "Dinner" the child might be provided a visual model of the expected sequence and then asked to walk through that sequence with his family. This would be done without the introduction of difficult foods. Then, after the sequence became familiar, the new foods could be systematically introduced to the child.

- *Have an EXIT strategy*—When beginning the generalization process it will be important for the treatment team to work with the family to plan for possible challenges. This will include the proactive supports that can be developed to help ensure success, but should also include a plan for what to do if there are problems in the moment. This should include procedures for prompting appropriate adaptive skills for choice making and refusals. For example, when the generalization food is refused, the child can be prompted to make an alternate choice and, minimally, use positive functional communication skills to navigate the situation. This will allow the family to limit challenging behavior while planning with the feeding clinicians about how to deal with the refusal of the target food.

Generalizing to School

As the child begins to become more comfortable with accepting foods and practice opportunities at home, the team will begin to expand food introduction into different settings, including school, community outings, and meals with extended family members and caregivers. The feeding team will likely develop a plan that incorporates practice trials of mastered foods into the school setting first, as the instruction methods should be consistent with the teaching strategies that have already been established within the academic setting. The school personnel may wish to accompany the child during a feeding session to directly observe the training procedures. This will be helpful for the school team to directly observe the oral-motor techniques, amount of food presented, and the verbal prompts used to support the child's performance. The team will also have an opportunity to work with the data sheets for additional carryover. When the school team has received consultation from the outpatient feeding providers, the school team may be able to work on foods that are currently being addressed during active treatment, rather than just mastered foods. With this sup-

port, the school team can work in conjunction with the feeding team, and the advances that that child will make will consequently be greater and quicker.

While it is optimal to have the school team and the feeding team to work closely with one another, many school teams are unable to attend a feeding session and may rely on the family to be a conduit to the feeding program. In this manner, then, the family will work directly with the school teacher and paraprofessionals to generalize the feeding program. Without direct contact with the feeding team, it may be most appropriate for the school personnel to introduce foods that have been mastered in treatment and that have already been introduced and are accepted well at home. For example, if the child had been working on yogurt at the feeding clinic and at home, and ultimately mastered it both at the clinic and at home by self-feeding the yogurt with a spoon, the feeding team would recommend that this food be introduced into different settings, including the school. The family may have observed that when it was first introduced, their child would eat his yogurt when he was offered a chip after he had finished the container. They can share this type of observation with the school team to promote success. It may also be beneficial for the family to meet with the key school team members to provide a bridge between the feeding program performed at the outpatient clinic, practice at home, and the new practice trials to be implemented at school.

Generalizing to the Community

As progress is made, the family will want to move forward with practice in more and different settings. Families may identify other priority members of their extended family that they wish to include in the generalization process. A child may spend considerable time in the homes of others such as grandparents, babysitters, and neighbors. The feeding team can work with the family to assist with introduction of foods into these familiar settings. Again, the family may need to act as the conduit between the feeding team and these other settings to promote consistency across these environments. In this manner, the family can explicitly work with the other caregivers using foods that have been mastered both at the clinic and at home. Typically, the primary caregivers will need to provide clear directions to extended family members and friends on how to best support feeding. For example, if the family has set up expectations that meals should be eaten at the kitchen table then it might be very important that this expectation be maintained at Grandma and Grandpa's house (at least for a short while).

It can be helpful for parents to emphasize that gains made in feeding need to be treated as fragile for a period until mastery has been well established. This can help extended family members appreciate the importance of being consistent while practicing in different settings. Also, families may note that some caregivers are more highly "preferred" and that their child may perform more successfully with these caregivers or in these environments. To build upon these successes in these settings, families can consider using these specific environments to practice mastered foods and actually advance new foods.

As the child begins to practice feeding skills at home, school, and with other caregivers, families become cautiously optimistic and begin to ask the question of whether it's time to try going to restaurants with their child. With increased flexibility gained during treatment, the child will begin to accept more foods that are typically part of a children's dining menu. In addition, the child is beginning to learn important mealtime behaviors and expectations that will allow him to sit for longer periods of time while waiting for food to arrive. Also, he is learning to communicate his needs with the appropriate language.

During feeding therapy, it will be important for the child to try different types of the same foods for generalization. For example, if macaroni and cheese was mastered in the feeding clinic, the team should explore different brands, shapes, and colors of macaroni and cheese so that the child will accept this food in many different forms of presentation. It will be helpful for the family and team to prioritize foods that are commonly served in restaurants as part of the targeted foods during intervention. If the family has a particular restaurant that they would like to frequent, the team can explore various options of that specific menu to determine targeted foods. Exploring restaurants and menu choices will also be a critical component if the family plans a vacation. With this advanced planning, these offered foods can be targeted during feeding intervention.

Dealing with the Unexpected

The process of generalizing skills requires family members to work collaboratively with treatment team members in order to guide, in a systematic fashion, skill expansion. This, however, is rarely a fully linear process. As gains are made, family members will come to feel more comfortable with taking risks. In many instances, a child with a feeding disorder will also begin to take risks and explore foods in a spontaneous fashion. Comprehensive family-system supports can be best employed with the development of a plan for coping with unplanned events. Here, we refer to the coping strategies for the adults supporting the individual with food restrictions. For example, what will the plan be for helping to redirect a negative reaction after a child tastes a new food for the first time? Alternatively, what is the plan for prompting a coping response when a child is given an unexpected demand by a grandparent who had heard tell of the wonderful progress during participation in a structured feeding treatment?

Given the importance of feeding interventions and the complexities of these introduced by the sensory and social features of the natural environment, it is always important that primary caregivers have a "Plan B" strategy for dealing with the unexpected. This will help prevent against any negative associations created by inadvertent forays into generalization that were unplanned and received with great difficulty. Typically, this will mean that the clinical team provides the family with recommendations of the best "go-to" prompts to provide to the child. For example, a "go-to" strategy may be to prompt functional language such as "Not now. Later," or "Can I pick something different?" This allows the family to have a consistent strategy for coping with the unexpected. This strategy should be used consistently with the child in order to ensure that as many difficult situations as possible end with a functional and highly effective response.

Supporting the Generalization Process

Generalization of gains made during structured feeding treatment is, arguably, the most essential feature of appropriate intervention. Without strong generalization it will be impossible for the child to experience sustainable gains. That is, the progress made in structured treatment may live primarily there. In the end, this will leave the child without the capacity to experience long term improvements in health. It is essential that any feeding team be prepared to support the family and entire support system with promoting generalization. As has been discussed previously, this begins with a process of establishing

home practice. This, however, is only the first step toward successful generalization. Gains must move with the child from one setting to the next, with the child demonstrating independence in all areas. This includes the social and adaptive skills associated with feeding such as expressing preferences, asking for assistance, tolerating sights and smells, and sharing mealtimes with others while seated.

As a child makes stable gains with foods during treatment, the team should immediately begin conversations about generalizing these to other environments. This will allow for the child to have immediate practice with skills across diverse settings and with different people. Further, this provides essential opportunities for the team to study barriers to generalization that will require specific supports. Once a comprehensive process for generalizing skills has been established, all members of the support team will need to maintain consistent dialogue and share data in order to ensure that success follows for the child.

The following are some tips to help set the stage for successful generalization:

- ***Know what tastes good to the child***—As the child starts to eat more and more foods, pay attention to those that become highly preferred. This will help to identify preferences and guide the selection of next foods. For example, if the child begins to eat blueberry yogurt, you may explore other berry flavors or foods with similar tastes to support generalization.

- ***Make good choices***—Select new foods to introduce based on an understanding of the child's preferences and the expectations of the setting. For example, when selecting foods to generalize to school, it may be necessary to pick only those that can be carried in a lunch bag and are able to be eaten with full independence.

- ***Know where to start***—Select a first setting for embedding practice and then move forward. For every child, the first steps toward generalizing foods will be different. Families should select initial practice environments that the child is in frequently, have a predictable schedule, and have adult support to help with skill transfer.

- ***Start easy***—To help with generalization, select the foods that are mastered, preferred, and appropriate for the setting.

- ***Adapt the environment***—Identify any necessary modifications to the environment to help support generalization. For example, you may carry over tools from treatment, such as a token board or other incentive system, to new environments in order to help build motivation and maintain some consistency. Also, you may adapt the environment by minimizing distractors that could limit initial success, such as strong smells or visual distractors.

- **Communicate with everyone involved**—Train other adults on the generalization process
- **Know what worked**—Be prepared to incorporate previously applied supports, such as visuals, into the natural environment. For example, if a child has practiced using a "First-Then" system when in treatment (e.g., "First take a bite of bagel, then one minute on the iPad"), you could implement this same strategy in the generalization setting.
- **Be ready**—Have a "Plan B" for coping with the unexpected. For example, a team may decide that when first attempting to generalize a food that has been mastered in treatment, if the child refuses, they will immediately offer a choice to do something easier with the food (e.g., smelling the food or touching it to his lips) in order to increase the likelihood of success with practice outside of treatment. Then the team will review the generalization barrier, having a conversation about the challenges experienced outside of the treatment setting, and develop a plan for trying again for independent eating.

8 Promoting Long-Term Healthy Eating: How Do We Know This is Working?

Mealtimes have long been a struggle for Zoey's family, but she is starting to feel cautiously optimistic. Riley, her five-year-old son with autism, has expanded his repertoire of food to include meats, pastas, fruits, and even previously-dreaded vegetables! Her friends have even her told her that Riley eats healthier foods than most other five-year-olds. Riley has not only expanded the repertoire of foods that he will eat, he will now go out to dinner with his family. Granted, there are only a few meals that he will select off of the children's menu, but this is a monumental step forward from where the family was a year ago. The family has even booked a trip to Disney for vacation, something they had talked about for years, but were unable to act upon due to Riley's severely restricted eating habits.

Riley was diagnosed at three years old with an autism spectrum disorder after presenting with significant behavioral challenges and language delays. While his language improved with therapy, his behavioral challenges persisted and influenced his ability to remain in a chair during meals. Additionally, Riley had rigid rules around the foods that he would eat, utensils and plates that he would accept, and even foods that his family members could eat in his presence. After fifteen months of treatment at an outpatient feeding clinic, Riley has expanded his food repertoire to more than forty-five foods, including foods from all of the food groups. He used to gag at the presentation of new foods, but even this has stopped. Zoey initially used the skills that she was taught during treatment to facilitate specific practice feeding sessions at home, but now she incorporates the foods that Riley has mastered into more typical family meals.

During this process, Zoey found that it was difficult to keep track of all of the foods that Riley mastered, and if he didn't practice eating them regularly, he was less likely to choose them for a meal. Not wanting Riley to lose newly gained foods, his treatment providers suggested using a box that contained cards with the names of all of the foods that Riley eats, dividing them by meal type, and using this as a way to keep track of the foods that he eats. Once a food has been selected during the week, the card gets moved to the back of the stack. This has allowed Zoey to monitor the foods that Riley eats and it even helps guide her grocery shopping list.

During the most recent feeding clinic appointment, the team told Zoey that Riley had made such significant gains that it was time to discuss termination of treatment. They reviewed his progress, including the oral-motor advances and the absence of a gag reflex with both the sight and physical presentation of new foods. They noted his gains in acceptance of foods across all the food groups and the fact that he now eats them in many different settings. They discussed the many times that Riley requested foods that they hadn't even tried in treatment while he was grocery shopping with his mom and how he ate those foods independently at home.

Zoey agreed with their observations of Riley's progress but was extremely reluctant to discontinue treatment. She appreciated the team's behavioral strategies that not only improved his mealtime participation, but also behavior at home and in the community. She was hesitant to stop treatment as she was afraid that Riley would lose the foods that he mastered and would revert back to his old habits of refusal. How did she know that Riley was ready to stop treatment? How would she manage continuing to introduce new foods without the support of the team that she and Riley had grown so close to in the past year?

The process of addressing feeding disorders begins with careful treatment that is guided by rigorous assessment procedures. This expands to a generalization process that helps the child master necessary feeding skills in natural environments. From here, families and clinicians must address questions of mastery and readiness to terminate treatment. Feeding disorders are often learned over the course of years and can require ongoing treatment in order to resolve the primary issues. Furthermore, the process of addressing not only food acceptance but also the related adaptive skill deficits (e.g., coping with change, choice making, and tolerating demands) can extend the total treatment process. By the time families are prepared for comprehensively generalizing skills across environments there are likely many questions about the long-term support needs of their child and the likelihood that the child will require ongoing help. This can bring forward many concerns for both families and treatment teams regarding decision making for terminating treatment. Typically, when addressing long-term sustainability of the gains made during a feeding treatment, families must consider the likelihood that without ongoing services their child may lose skills. Comprehensive treatments to address feeding disorders must grapple with such issues of sustainability in order to help ensure that, upon termination, patients are fully prepared for success.

The discussion about termination of treatment begins on the first day of treatment. It is critical to define the specific long-term goals of the intervention in the early stages of the process. Typically, parents are so overwhelmed with what seems like an impossible goal of eating new foods that often times their goals are less specific and very small. It is helpful for the treatment team and the family to sit together and thoughtfully plan long-term goals that incorporate adequate nutritional objectives, cooperation during mealtime routines, and generalization of these skills to a variety of settings. By defining these parameters specific to the child and the family's needs and priorities, progress can be measured objectively during each phase of the treatment process. Subsequently, discharge planning can be discussed with attainment of each objective.

Often, families and the treatment team consider foods from each of the major food groups as potential long-term goals. Families can discuss additional nutritional needs with their pediatrician or a dietician, particularly if there are any food allergies or dietary restrictions. It will also be important to consider the variety settings in which the child will eat these foods, such as home, school, a day care center, or even Disney World on a long-awaited family vacation. As mealtimes are typically a social event, social skills can also be incorporated into long-term objective planning. Having a child sit through an entire meal at the table, communicate needs and preferences effectively and appropriately, and tolerate the variety of sights and smells of various foods are realistic—yet often only dreamed about—goals that many families will select as their end plan for a feeding program.

Additionally, the smaller steps that lead to the larger goals can also be defined during the early phases of the intervention process. The attainment in fluency of such oral-motor skills as moving food from one side of the mouth to other, incorporating a more mature chewing pattern while eating, and removing food from a spoon with adequate lip control are all small components of larger feeding and eating skills. When these components are achieved, the child will demonstrate better food management abilities and be able to eat a wider variety of foods and food textures.

As the child progresses through feeding treatment, attainment of the defined goals and objectives will be measured by the feeding team. These and other measures of success during the treatment process will indicate that the child is ready to be discharged from intervention. Each of the following milestones will be important points for the treatment team and family to consider as they highlight gains and help focus the dialogue regarding appropriate times to fade interventions.

1. The child is able to share complete meals independently with her family.

By the end of the intervention process, mealtimes will have evolved into far less stressful events for the child and her family. The child and her family will have initially practiced small "tasting times" when feeding intervention started. Building upon these successes, the family will be able to increase the duration of time spent at the table, eventually introducing mastered foods as snacks and later into small meals. As the child expands her repertoire of foods to include foods of various consistencies, she will ultimately improve her oral-motor abilities and overall tolerance to sustained chewing efforts. This will allow the child to eat for longer periods of time without fatigue.

Over time, improved tolerance to the various sensory aspects of food, i.e., the visual presentation and the smells of certain foods, will assist in having the child remain seated at the table without adverse reaction. The family will also closely examine the physical environment of the meal, assessing that the child is stable in her chair and that her feet are supported to maintain efficient trunk stability to remain upright for an extended period of time. By remaining at the table for an entire meal, the child and family can share a rich and rewarding social opportunity that transcends far beyond the actual meal itself.

2. The child can use feeding and feeding-related skills in many different settings.

The skills addressed in feeding treatment can, at times, feel isolated from other parts of the child's life. It is essential that all new abilities be generalized across environments, as was discussed in previous chapters. This includes not only eating foods but all the related social and communication skills that are associated with feeding. As families and treatment teams consider terminating treatment, it is helpful to conduct observations of the child in multiple environments to see if skills persist and are functionally used. A child who can successfully use a skill will be able to apply it, flexibly, in multiple locations, with various people, and with different foods and materials (for example tables, plates, and utensils).

It is helpful to slowly present the child with new situations and observe if the skills are independently applied. To do this, the team should make sure that all the expectations for successful use of skills are clear for the child and the adults involved. Then the family can identify a new setting and allow the child an opportunity to independently apply the skills. If the child is fully flexible with the skills used then the child can be progressively exposed to new settings with increased expectations for success. If the child needs support, the adults must be ready to move in, provide that support, and ensure success. From this point, the team can develop naturalistic strategies to ensure that independence is achieved before new expectations are presented.

3. The child can effectively communicate needs and preferences regarding feeding.

Effective functional communication skills are essential if a person is to independently navigate exploring new foods, eating, and sharing in meals with others. Functional communication training to expand the child's ability to communicate needs and preferences should be considered essential to effective feeding treatment. Certainly, this will require the team to coordinate with other educators and therapists to ensure consistency. Once this has been achieved it is crucial that family members be guided to reinforce the use of successful communication skills in all feeding settings and, importantly, construct the environment to encourage frequent skill use. This can include building choices into meals as well as presenting low and high preference foods for the child to select from using successful communication. Eventually this will also mean presenting the child with low preference foods, but foods that the family expects will be eaten as part of the meal, and likewise, helping the child to communicate effectively and to tolerate this moment.

A child who is successful with communication skills will be able to spontaneously label preferences, make choices, request help, appropriately refuse, and select functional alternatives. Often as gains are made during treatment there is a tendency to be extremely consistent at home. The task of preparing the child to terminate treatment is to build in opportunities to navigate, using strong communication abilities, a variety of feeding scenarios.

4. New foods can be introduced and mastered easily.

As treatment progresses, the child learns the process by which new foods are introduced and becomes comfortable with the predictable steps of new food introduction. Her oral-motor skills have improved and her overall ability to manage foods in her mouth has become more proficient. She tolerates the sensory aspects of different foods more easily and is able to effectively express preferences for foods.

By the end of treatment, the team will recognize that new foods can be introduced and progressed through the hierarchy far more quickly than at the start of intervention. They may notice that the child can begin a new food and master it within the same treatment session or only with a few practice sessions at home as well. The team may also be able to trial new foods higher up on the hierarchy by the end of the treatment process—stepping forward—as the child gains more comfort with her own feeding abilities. In this manner, then, foods with a more complex consistency can be introduced in their natural form without modification to the consistency or presentation of the food itself, and be progressed towards mastery quickly. Families will identify that by the end of treatment, the foods that they are selecting are, in fact, part of the very meals that they are serving at home.

5. The child asks for a taste of foods that she has never tried before.

Not all children will independently do this without direct teaching; however, when this skill is present, it is a good indicator of success. Throughout the intervention process, the feeding team will address improving tolerance to all sensory aspects of selected foods. The team will also focus on oral-motor management skills so that the child can more effectively manage foods of increasing complexity. If the child had initially expressed atypical reactions to the sight of a new food or the feeling of the food in her mouth, these reactions would be explicitly addressed during feeding intervention.

These responses might include gagging, spitting, or facial grimacing. As these atypical responses decrease during intervention with the use of a hierarchical presentation of each new food, the child will naturally become more comfortable with the eating process itself and begin to accept new foods with greater ease. By the end of the feeding intervention, the child may look to an adult's plate and seek out a food item that she has never tried before and taste it. She may also see a food advertised on TV and request that food item of her caregivers. Additionally, she may also accept a new snack presented by her teachers at school without difficulty.

6. The child does not lose previously accepted foods due to infrequent practice.

As treatment progresses, there are likely to be many foods introduced and mastered by the child. Over time, there will be so many foods that daily or weekly practice with each of them becomes a challenge. As an indicator of long-term health, the team should look to see if foods that have not been practiced for some time can be successfully reintroduced and accepted. It is extremely common that over the course of a year some of the foods eaten by a family change. Successful eaters will be able to navigate these changes. In this respect, a comprehensive approach to feeding treatment must consider sustainability. It will be important that foods need not be reintroduced and systematically faded in over time but rather that the child can independently maintain familiarity and tolerance of them. In some instances, teams need to develop specific intervention features to help build endurance in this regard. This can include placing foods into long-term rotations or maintaining reinforcement systems at home for tolerating foods that haven't been eaten in a while, until the child's skills expand. Teams must support the child to make these long-term gains as they move forward with fading treatment in order to facilitate lifelong health.

7. The child can master new foods that caregivers introduce outside of treatment.

Structured feeding interventions rely heavily upon a strong collaboration between the clinical team and the family. As has been discussed in previous chapters, this involves building structure into the entire day to support skill growth. Over time, however, this structure fades and the family should be able to move forward with new foods

independently. This often happens naturally as the child begins requesting tastes of new foods or as caregivers feel comfortable pushing forward with new explorations.

As the child's independence improves, it will be common for the family to relax concerns about feeding and to more seamlessly integrate the child into meals and other food-related family routines. It is common for the family of a child who is almost ready to complete treatment to arrive at the feeding session with a story about a new food that was independently eaten, perhaps at a family dinner at a relative's home where a grandparent simply offered a food and the child happy took it. Also, school environments can present many opportunities for new foods to be presented without highly structured supports. Teams commonly observe a child, who was once highly rigid with respect to the foods she would taste, accepting tastes of snacks from friends or accepting a birthday treat without difficultly. As the natural environment takes over with the presentation of new foods, the teams can feel comfortable fading treatment.

8. Oral-motor skills are well established.

At the beginning of the feeding process, the child may have exhibited compromised oral-motor skills that affected her overall successful management of food itself. Due to food restrictions, the child does not try foods of increasing complexity and misses practice opportunities to develop these necessary foundation skills for chewing and overall oral management. Ultimately, the child may avoid those foods that require more oral-motor work due to inefficiencies, further restricting her food repertoire.

During the course of intervention, the team will address any underlying oral-motor deficits and may even assign homework practice to address such skills as lip pursing, tongue mobility, and chewing. These homework skills may be introduced into the school environment as well to offer additional practice opportunities. Gradually, foods with increasing consistency complexity will be introduced into the child's repertoire, allowing for additional integration of these oral-motor skills in the most practical of activities. By the end of the treatment process, the food items themselves may become the only tool needed to continue to develop and refine the child's oral-motor abilities.

9. There are no ongoing nutritional concerns due to feeding limitations.

At the start of treatment, families often report significant concerns about their child's nutritional status due to a highly restrictive feeding repertoire. Very often, diets can be highly unbalanced because only certain types of foods are accepted. For example, many children begin treatment with a select group of crunchy carbohydrates that they will eat, one or two meats, a few dairy products, but virtually no fruits or vegetables. Throughout treatment, the ongoing dialogue about what foods should be introduced next will help address building a healthy dietary profile for the child. At times, it will be appropriate for the child's pediatrician or dietician to review her progress and make any necessary recommendations for foods to introduce. This will be especially important for children with food allergies and other dietary restrictions. By the end of the treatment process, the family should be comfortable that the foods accepted by their child compose a healthy diet.

Indicators of Success and Long-Term Gains:

- The child is able to share complete meals independently with her family.
- The child can use feeding and feeding-related skills in many different settings.
- The child can effectively communicate needs and preferences regarding feeding.
- New foods can be introduced and mastered easily.
- The child asks for tastes of foods that she has never tried before.
- The child does not lose previously accepted foods due to infrequent practice.
- The child can master new foods that caregivers introduce outside of treatment.
- Oral-motor skills are well established.
- There are no ongoing nutrition concerns due to feeding limitations.

Conclusion

The question of knowing when to terminate treatment is always complicated. Feeding issues are often much more extensive than refusing to eat a diverse group of foods. They encompass the social and adaptive skills that are necessary for successful eating. Skills such as being able to indicate preferences, knowing how to follow a mealtime routine, and coping with difficult demands are essential to any individual's success with respect to feeding. Without both flexible and diverse levels of food acceptance and strong social and adaptive skills, a person is likely to experience lifelong limitations with feeding. Appropriate treatment will therefore apply the necessary emphasis on all relevant abilities and follow each of these to generalization.

Treatment must follow an evidence-based approach with data collected on all interventions to ensure that treatment gains are made in the most efficient and effective fashion possible. This approach will allow all members of the treatment team to share in an objective review of gains, and more effectively contribute to decision making. Data collection should occur across every setting, though certainly the style of the collection procedures will vary based upon the settings (for example, a protocol used in therapy will be adjusted substantially for home use). As treatment begins, the team must consider generalization as early as possible. This means establishing a way for family members to help with daily skill practice and report to clinicians on the child's progress.

The question of terminating treatment is considered early on by the family and treatment team as they set goals for intervention. However, as the time to actively move forward with fading treatment arrives, questions often emerge regarding the viability of the child's gains and the need to continue with active intervention. The features of sustainable progress described above should be considered by all team members in order to help evaluate gains and make recommendations for fading or terminating treatment. Typically, the process of discontinuing a treatment as comprehensive as feeding interventions occurs over an interval where supports are systematically pulled back and the child's progress is carefully monitored for stable gains.

The goals initially set during assessment are reviewed throughout the course of treatment and at the point of termination, the entire team should be comfortable with the child's progress and long-term outlook.

A child who can share in a meal with her family and peers, and who can tolerate the myriad social and sensory stimuli of that meal, has innumerable opportunities not only for strong physical health but also for positive social and emotional well-being. Over the course of treatment, the initial steps toward generalization move forward to incorporate more people, diverse settings, and different types of foods. The goal of any comprehensive feeding program is to nurture a flexible and strong skill repertoire that will remain stable for a lifetime of healthy eating.

Resources & References

Ahearn, W. H. (2002). Effect of two methods of introducing foods during feeding treatment on acceptance of previously rejected items. *Behavioral Interventions, 17,* 111-127.

Ahearn, W. H., Castine, T., Nault, K., & Green, G. (2001). An assessment of food acceptance in children with autism or Pervasive Developmental Disorder: Not Otherwise Specified. *Journal of Autism and Developmental Disorders, 31*(5), 505-511.

Ahearn, W. H., Kerwin, M. E., Eicher, P. S., & Lukens, C. T. (2001). An ABAC comparison of two intensive interventions for food refusal. *Behavior Modification,* 25, 385-405.

Ahearn, W. H., Kerwin, M. E., Eicher, P. S., Shantz, J., & Swearingin, W. (1996). An alternating treatments comparison of two intensive interventions for food refusal. *Journal of Applied Behavioral Analysis, 29,* 321-332.

Amato, J. & Slavin, D. (1998). A preliminary investigation of oromotor function in young verbal and nonverbal children with autism. *Infant-Toddler Intervention, 8,*(2), 175-184.

American Psychiatric Association. (2000). Diagnostic and statistical manual of mental disorders (4th ed., text rev.). Washington, DC: Author.

Babbit, R. L., Shore, B. A., Smith, M., Williams, K. E., & Coe, D. A. (2001). Stimulus fading in the treatment of ADIPSIA. *Behavioral Interventions, 16,* 197-207.

Bachmeyer, M. H., Piazza, C. C., Fredrick, L. D., Reed, G. K., Rivas, K. D., & Kadey, H. J. (2009). Functional analysis and treatment of multiply controlled inappropriate mealtime behavior. *Journal of Applied Behavior Analysis, 42*, 641-658.

Baranek, G. T. (2002). Efficacy of sensory and motor interventions for children with autism. *Journal of Autism and Developmental Disabilities, 32*(5), 397-422.

Binnendyk, L. & Lucyshyn, J. M. (2009). A family-centered positive behavior support approach to the amelioration of food refusal behavior. *Journal of Positive Behavior Intervention, 11*, 47-62.

Borrero, C. S., Woods, J. N., Borrero, J. C., Masler, E. A., & Lesser, A. D. (2010). Descriptive analysis of pediatric food refusal and acceptance. *Journal of Applied Behavior Analysis, 43*, 71-88.

Boshart, C. A. (1998). *Oral-motor analysis and remediation techniques.* Temecula, CA: Speech Dynamics.

Bregman, J. D., Zager, D., & Gerdtz, J. (2005). Behavioral interventions. In F. R. Volkmar, R. Paul, A. Klin, & D. Cohen (Eds.), *Handbook of autism and pervasive developmental disorders, 3rd ed.* (pp. 5-41). New Jersey: Wiley.

Burklow, K. A., Phelps, A. N., Schultz, J. R., McConnell, K., & Colin, R. (1998). Classifying complex pediatric feeding disorders. *Journal of Pediatric Gastroenterology & Nutrition, 2*, 143-147.

Casey, S. D., Cooper-Brown, L. J., Wacker, D. P., & Rankin, B. E. (2006). The use of descriptive analysis to identify and manipulate schedules of reinforcement in the treatment of food refusal. *Journal of Behavioral Education, 15*, 41-52.

Chung, K. & Kahng, S. (2006). Pediatric feeding disorders. In J. E. Fisher & W. T. O'Donohue (Eds.), *Practitioner's guide to evidence-based psychotherapy* (pp. 514-523). New York: Springer.

Clark, H. (2003). Neuromuscular treatments for speech and swallowing: A tutorial. *American Journal of Speech-Language Pathology, 12*, 400-415.

Cooper, J. O., Heron, T. E., & Heward, W. L. (2007). *Applied behavior analysis*. Upper Saddle River, NJ: Prentice Hall.

Cooper, L. J., Wacker, D. P., Brown, K., Mccomas, J. J., Peck, S. M., Drew, J., et al. (1999). Use of a concurrent operants paradigm to evaluate positive reinforcers during treatment of food refusal. *Behavior Modification, 23*, 3-40.

Cooper, L. J., Wacker, D. P., McComas, J. J., Brown, K., Peck, S. M., Richman, D., et al. (1995). Use of component analyses to identify active variables in treatment packages for children with feeding disorders. *Journal of Applied Behavior Analysis, 28*, 139-153.

Cornish, E. (1998). A balanced approach towards healthy eating in autism. *Journal of Human Nutrition and Dietetics, 11*, 501-509.

Couriel, J. M., Bisset, R., Miller, R., Thomas, A., & Clarke, M. (1993). Assessment of feeding problems in neurodevelopmental handicap: A team approach. *Archives of Disease in Childhood, 69*, 609-613.

De Moor, J., Didden, R., & Korzilius, H. (2007). Behavioural treatment of severe food refusal in five toddlers with developmental disabilities. *Child: Care, Health and Development, 33*, 670-676.

Eckman, N., Williams, K. E., Riegel, K., & Paul, C. (2008). Teaching chewing: A structured approach. *American Journal of Occupational Therapy, 62*, 514-521.

Flanagan, M. A. (2008). *Improving speech and eating skills in children with autism spectrum disorders: An oral-motor program for home and school.* Shawnee Mission, KS: Autism Asperger Publishing Company.

Galensky, T. L., Miltenberger, R. G., Stricker, J. M., & Garlinghouse, M. A. (2001). Functional assessment and treatment of mealtime behavior problems. *Journal of Positive Behavior Interventions, 3*, 211-224.

Girolami, P. A., Boscoe, J. H., & Roscoe, N. (2007). Decreasing expulsions by a child with a feeding disorder: Using a brush to present and re-present food. *Journal of Applied Behavior Analysis, 40*, 749-753.

Girolami, P. A. & Scotti, J. R. (2001). Use of analog functional analysis in assessing the function of mealtime behavior problems. *Education and training in mental retardation and developmental disabilities, 36*, 207-223.

Gulotta, C. S., Piazza, C. C., Patel, M. R., & Layer, S. A. (2005). Using food redistribution to reduce packing in children with severe food refusal. *Journal of Applied Behavior Analysis, 38* (1), 39-50.

Hillman, H. L. (2006). Functional analysis and food refusal: A brief review. *The Behavior Analyst Today, 7*(1), 49-55.

Hogopian, L. P., Farrell, D. A., & Amari, A. (1996). Treating total liquid refusal with backward chaining and fading. *Journal of Applied Behavior Analysis*, 29, 573-575.

Iwata, B. A., Dorsey, M. F., Slifer, K. J., Bauman, K. E., & Richman, G. S. (1994). Toward a functional analysis of self-injury. *Journal of Applied Behavior Analysis*, 27, 197-209. (Reprinted from *Analysis and Intervention in Developmental Disabilities, 2*, 3-20, 1982). *27*, 215-240.

Kahng, S., Boscoe, J. H., & Byrne, S. (2003). The use of an escape contingency and a token economy to increase food acceptance. *Journal of Applied Behavior Analysis, 36*, 349-353.

Keen, D. V. (2008). Childhood autism, feeding problems and failure to thrive in early infancy: Seven case studies. *European Child & Adolescent Psychiatry, 17*, 209-216.

Kerwin, M. E. & Eicher, P. S. (2004). Behavioral intervention and prevention of feeding difficulties in infants and toddlers. *Journal of Early Intensive Behavioral Intervention, 1*, 129-140.

Kerwin, M. E., Eicher, P. S., & Gelsinger, J. (2005). Parental report of eating problems and gastrointestinal symptoms in children with pervasive developmental disorders. *Children's Health Care, 34*, 221-234.

Kuschner, E., Bennetto, L., & Silverman, L. (2005). Gustatory function and food preferences in high-functioning autism [Abstract]. International Meeting for Autism Research, (Abstract No. P3A.1.13), 118–119.

Levin, L. & Carr, E. G. (2001). Food selectivity and problem behavior in children with developmental disabilities: Analysis and intervention. *Behavior Modification, 25*, 443-470.

Linscheid, T. R. (2006). Behavioral treatments for pediatric feeding disorders. *Behavior Modification, 30*, 6-23.

Luiselli, J. K. & Luiselli, T. E. (1995). A behavior analysis approach toward chronic food refusal in children with gastrostomy-tube dependency. *Topics in Early Childhood Special Education, 15*, 1-18.

Luiselli, J. K., Ricciardi, J. N., & Gilligan, K. (2005). Liquid fading to establish milk consumption by a child with autism. *Behavioral Interventions, 20*, 155-163.

Mace, F. C., Hock, M. L., Lalli, J. S., West, B. J., Belfiore, P., Pinter, E., et al. (1998). Behavioral momentum in the treatment of noncompliance. *Journal of Applied Behavior Analysis, 21*, 123-141.

McCartney, E. J., Anderson, C. M., & English, C. L. (2005). Effect of brief clinic-based training on the ability of caregivers to implement escape extinction. *Journal of Positive Behavior Interventions, 7*, 18-32.

Mueller, M. M., Piazza, C. C., Patel, M. R., & Pruett, A. (2004). Increasing variety of foods consumed by blending nonpreferred foods into preferred foods. *Journal of Applied Behavior Analysis, 37*, 159-170.

Munk, D. D. & Repp, A. C. (1994). Behavioral assessment of feeding problems of individuals with severe disabilities. *Journal of Applied Behavior Analysis, 27*, 241-250.

Patel, M. R., Piazza, C. C., Santana, C. M., & Volkert, V. M. (2002). An evaluation of food type and texture in the treatment of a feeding problem. *Journal of Applied Behavior Analysis, 35*(2), 183-186.

Penrod, B., Wallace, M. D., Reagon, K., Betz, A., & Higbee, T. S. (2010). A component analysis of a parent-conducted multi-component treatment for food selectivity. *Behavioral Interventions, 25*, 207-228.

Piazza, C. C., Fisher, W. W., Brown, K. A., Shore, B. A., Patel, M. R., Katz, R. M., et al. (2003). Functional analysis of inappropriate mealtime behaviors. *Journal of Applied Behavior Analysis, 36*, 187-204.

Piazza, C. C., Roane, H. S., & Kadey, H. J. (2009). Treatment of pediatric feeding disorders. In J. L. Matson, F. Andrasik, & M. L. Matson (Eds.), *Treating childhood psychopathology and developmental disabilities* (pp. 435-444). New York: Springer.

Powers, K. P. (1996). Oral-motor and behavioral treatment of feeding disorders in autism: A case study. Unpublished master's thesis, San Jose State University, San Jose, CA.

Rivas, K. D., Piazza, C. C., Patel, M. R, & Bachmeyer, M. H. (2010). Spoon distance fading with and without escape extinction as treatment for food refusal. *Journal of Applied Behavior Analysis, 43*, 673-683.

Schreck, K. A., Williams, K., & Smith, A. F. (2004). A comparison of eating behaviors between children with and without autism. *Journal of Autism and Developmental Disorders, 34*(4), 433-438.

Sharp, W. G., Jaquess, D. L., Morton, J. F., & Herzinger, C. V. (2010). Pediatric feeding disorders: A quantitative synthesis of treatment outcomes. *Clinical Child and Family Psychological Review, 13*, 348-365.

Volkmar, F. R. & Klin, A. (2005). Issues in the classification of autism and related conditions. In F. R. Volkmar, R. Paul, A. Klin, & D. Cohen (Eds.), *Handbook of autism and pervasive developmental disorders, 3rd ed.* (pp. 5-41). New Jersey: Wiley.

Williams, P. G., Dalrymple, N., & Neal, J. (2000). Eating habits of children with autism. *Pediatric Nursing, 26*, 259-264.

Index

About the Author

Dr. Mark Palmieri is a licensed psychologist and board certified behavior analyst. He is currently the Director of School Consultation Services and the Co-Director of the Feeding Clinic at the Center for Children with Special Needs in Glastonbury, CT. He has trained teams in comprehensive program development for individuals with intensive needs and has lectured nationally and internationally on evidence-based interventions, including specialized treatments to address feeding challenges.

Kristen Powers has been practicing as an occupational therapist for over 23 years. She currently serves as the Coordinator of Rehabilitative Services, as well as Co-Director of the Feeding Clinic at the Center for Children with Special Needs in Glastonbury, CT. She has lectured on feeding challenges and sensory-motor issues in children with ASD both in the US and abroad.